S0-BMS-520

For Women
Pocket Monologues
from
Shakespeare

FOR WOMEN
POCKET MONOLOGUES
from
SHAKESPEARE

Edited by Dick Dotterer

Dramaline Publications

Copyright © 1997, Dramaline Publications. All Rights Reserved. Printed in the United States of America.

No part of this publication may be reproduced or transmitted in any form or by any means, electronic or mechanical, including photocopy, recording, or any information storage and retrieval system now known or to be invented, without permission in writing from the publisher, except by a reviewer who wishes to quote brief passages in connection with a review written for inclusion in a magazine, newspaper, or for broadcast. Material in this publication may be utilized for workshop, audition, and classwork purposes without royalty consideration. If, however, the material is presented individually, or in total, before an audience where admission is charged, royalty payment is required. Contact the publisher for applicable rates.

Dramaline Publications, 36-851 Palm View Road
Rancho Mirage, CA 92270

Library of Congress Cataloging-in-Publication Data

Shakespeare, William, 1564-1616.
  For Women: Pocket Monologues from Shakespeare/
edited by Dick Dotterer
      p.   cm.
  ISBN 0-940669-38-2
  1. Women—Drama.   2. Monologues.   I. Dotterer, Dick.
II. Title.
PR2768.D57   1997
822.3'3—dc21   97-45806

Cover design by John Sabel

CONTENTS

THE COMEDIES:

Two Gentlemen of Verona, Silvia   1
Two Gentlemen of Verona, Julia   3
The Taming of the Shrew, Katharina   6
Love's Labour's Lost, Princess   8
A Midsummer Night's Dream, Titania   11
A Midsummer Night's Dream, Helena   15
A Midsummer Night's Dream, Helena   17
As You Like It, Rosalind   21
As You Like It, Rosalind   24
As You Like It, Phebe   26
The Merry Wives of Windsor, M. Quickly   28
The Comedy of Errors, Adriana   32
The Merchant of Venice, Portia   35
Twelfth Night, Viola   39
All's Well That Ends Well, Helena   41

THE TRAGEDIES:

Romeo and Juliet, Nurse	45
Romeo and Juliet, Juliet	48
Romeo and Juliet, Juliet	50
Julius Caesar, Portia	52
Hamlet, Ophelia	55
Hamlet, Queen Gertrude	57
Othello, Desdemona	59
Othello, Desdemona	61
Titus Andronicus, Tamora	63
Macbeth, Lady Macbeth	66
King Lear, Goneril	68
King Lear, Cordelia	70
Antony and Cleoparta, Cleopatra	73
Antony and Cleopatra, Cleopatra	75

THE ROMANCES:

Pericles, Dionyza   77
Pericles, Marina   79
Cymbeline, The Queen   82
Cymbeline, Imogen   86
Cymbeline, Imogen   89
The Tempest, Miranda   93
The Tempest, Miranda   94
Troilus and Cressida, Cressida   97
All's Well That Ends Well, Helena   100
All's Well That Ends Well, Countess   101
Measure for Measure, Isabella   104

THE HISTORIES:

King Henry IV, Part I, Lady Percy 107
King Henry IV, Part II, Mistress Quickly 108
King Henry IV, Part II, Doll Tearsheet 111
King Henry V, Hostess 113
King Henry VI, Part II, Queen Margaret 115
King Henry VI, Part II, Queen Margaret 118
King Henry VI, Part III, Queen Margaret 122
King Henry VI, Part III, Queen Margaret 125
King Henry VIII, Queen Katherine 127
King Richard II, Duchess of York 131
King Richard III, Lady Anne 134
King Richard III, Lady Anne 137
King Richard III, Queen Margaret 139
King John, Constance 142
King John, Constance 146
King John, Constance 149

THE COMEDIES

The Two Gentlemen of Verona
SILVIA—ACT IV, SCENE 3

This is one of Shakespeare's earliest comedies, and his first romantic comedy. Moreover, it is one in which he began experimenting with characters and situations that would come to fuller blossom in his later, more produced, and richer comedies. Silvia is the daughter of the reigning duke of Milan. She is daring and she is witty (something Shakespeare seemed to admire in women, and qualities with which he endowed most of his heroines). Silvia is also in love with Valentine, a young gentleman from Verona attached for the time to the ducal court in Milan. Valentine returns her love. However, her father, the Duke, has other plans for Silvia, which includes her betrothal to a foolish nobleman named Thurio. The Duke's good opinion of Valentine is further thwarted by Proteus, Valentine's best friend, who also has designs on Silvia. But Silvia remains true to Valentine. The Duke banishes Valentine from Milan for trying to elope with Silvia. Silvia, however, is determined to disobey her father's orders to marry Thurio, and she intends to follow after Valentine in a clandestine fashion.

1

It is late at night, outside Silvia's chambers in the Duke's palace, and Silvia is meeting with another courtier, Sir Eglamour, whom she has asked to escort her to Mantua so she may be with her exiled love, Valentine.

SILVIA

Sir Eglamour, a thousand times good morrow.
O Eglamour, thou art a gentleman—
Think not I flatter, for I swear I do not—
Valiant wise, remorseful, well accomplish'd:
Thou art not ignorant what dear good will
I bear unto the banish'd Valentine,
Nor how my father would enforce me marry
Vain Thurio, whom my very soul abhors.
Thyself has loved; and I have heard thee say
No grief did ever come so near thy heart
As when thy lady and thy true love died,
Upon whose grave thou vow'dst pure chastity.
Sir Eglamour, I would to Valentine,
To Mantua, where I hear he makes abode;
And, for the ways are dangerous to pass,
I do desire thy worthy company,
Upon whose faith and honour I repose.
Urge not my father's anger, Eglamour,
But think upon my grief, a lady's grief,

And on the justice of my flying hence,
To keep me from a most unholy match,
Which heaven and fortune still rewards with plagues.
I do desire thee, even from a heart
As full of sorrows as the sea of sands,
To bear me company and go with me:
If not to hide what I have said to thee,
That I may venture to depart alone.
Good morrow, kind Sir Eglamour.

> [*Exeunt severally.*]

The Two Gentleman of Verona
JULIA—ACT IV, SCENE 4

*The role of Julia deserves a special footnote in the
history of Shakespeare's plays. She is the first of his
famous "breeches" roles. When Julia assumes the
disguise of a male page to follow after her lover,
Proteus, Shakespeare began the practice he was to
use to great effect in later plays. Since woman's roles
were played by adolescent boys and young men, it
was very convincing, not to say practical, to have
these boy-actors disguise themselves as boys!*

*Julia is a sweet and unselfish young woman who
is in love with Proteus, a young man who, as the story
progresses, turns into a treacherous and unpleasant
twerp. He turns his affections from Julia once he sees*

Silvia, who is in love with his best friend, Valentine.
And Proteus then plots to steal Silvia from Valentine.
But this doesn't deter Julia. In a situation that
foreshadows the Viola-Orsino relationship in Twelfth
Night, *Julia courts Silvia as a male page for Proteus.*
Of course, she is so convincing as a boy that Proteus
does not recognize her as the lady he left behind in
Verona, nor does Silvia suspect that Julia is another
female, let alone the hapless Julia herself.

Julia, in disguise, has just had an interview with
Silvia, an interview that has surprised Julia. As the
page, she has brought a letter to Silvia from Proteus,
along with the gift of a ring, the very ring which Julia
herself gave Proteus as a token when he left Verona.
Silvia knows about Proteus' jilting of Julia, and she
rejects both Proteus' written protestations and the
ring, saying that while Proteus' "false finger have
profaned the ring, /Mine shall not do his Julia so
much wrong." Silvia has just left the sorrowing and
disguised Julia alone with her reactions to this un-
usual and unexpected encounter.

JULIA

A virtuous gentlewoman, mild and beautiful!
I hope my master's suit will be but cold,
Since she respects my mistress' love so much.

Alas, how love can trifle with itself!
Here is her picture: let me see; I think,
If I had such a tire, this face of mine
Were full as lovely as is this of hers:
And yet the painter flatter'd her a little,
Unless I flatter with myself too much.
Her hair is auburn, mine is perfect yellow:
If that be all the difference in his love,
I'll get me such a colour'd periwig.
Her eyes are grey as glass, and so are mine:
Ay, but her forehead's low, and mine's high.
What should it be that he respects in her
But I can make respective in myself,
If this fond Love were not a blinded god?
Come, shadow, come, and take this shadow up,
For 'tis thy rival. O thou senseless form,
Thou shalt be worshipp'd, kiss'd, loved and adored!
And, were there sense in his idolatry,
My substance should be statue in thy stead.
I'll use thee kindly for thy mistress' sake,
That used me so; or else, by Jove I vow,
I should have scratch'd out your unseeing eyes,
To make my master out of love with thee!

[*Exit*]

5

The Taming of the Shrew
KATHARINA—ACT VI, SCENE 3

*Kate and Petruchio are Shakespeare's first pair of
unforgettable comic lovers, creations that entered
into the lexicons as named examples of such
relationships. Shakespeare had an outstanding
sympathy with his women characters, and an almost
uncanny understanding of them. It is one of the
distinguishing features of his plays—especially of his
comedies. But it must also be remembered that
Shakespeare's moral outlook was always conformist
and conservative. He was a normal family man (as
much as his profession would allow him, with his
family safely in Stratford), and his view was that of
the normal Elizabethan one. And the normal
Elizabethan view was that as dictated by St. Paul and
as interpreted by the Church of the time: women were
to be subject to their husbands, for the husband was
the head of the woman.*

*The originality of this farce is that Petruchio
"tames" his shrewish wife by comic means. They are
outwardly rough, but mitigated by an inward love, for
Petruchio really does love Katharina. (It is
interesting to note that from the text of the play,
Petruchio never strikes Kate, nor beats her, even
though she slaps him.) Kate is to be tamed in comic*

terms. She is to be bridled, like a spring colt, with firmness mixed with unmitigated love. The twist is, of course, that Kate falls in love with her husband, but she is too proud and too obstinate to admit it.

Katharina has been compared to a wasp. She is pert; she is quick; she is determined. And underneath all of her petticoats she may have—and she should have—a good heart, or the audience would lose all care for her. By Act IV, Petruchio's system of taming his wife is starting to show its effects. Kate has not been allowed to rest nor has she had a full mean since she has left her father's house and arrived at Petruchio's villa. She is at the point of exhaustion from frustration—a comic victim of the mistress killed with kindness, so to speak. At the moment, Kate is trying to persuade Petruchio's servant, Grumio, by any means, to bring her some food. She is starving.

KATHARINA

The more my wrong, the more his spite appears:
What, did he marry me to famish me?
Beggars, that come into my father's door,
Upon entreaty have a present alms;
If not, elsewhere they meet with chairty:
But I, who never knew how to entreat,
Nor never needed that I should entreat,

Am starved for meat, giddy for lack of sleep,
With oaths kept waking and with brawling fed:
And that which spites me more than all these wants,
He does it under the name of perfect love;
And who should say, if I should sleep or eat,
'Twere deadly sickness or else present death.
I prithee go and get me some repast;
I care not what, so it be some wholesome food.

Love's Labour's Lost
**PRINCESS OF FRANCE—ACT V,
SCENE 2**

*Love's Labour's Lost is, perhaps, Shakespeare's
most acutely personal play; and in it one finds his
high spirits and examples of his verbal cleverness.
One also finds the themes, situations, and characters
he would use again and again and develop into
greater roundness in his later plays, especially his romantic comedies. It is also a romantic comedy that
mixes scenes of pure farce with scenes of intricate
poetry and lyrical verse. And with this play,
Shakespeare also experimented with closing a
comedy of light-hearted gaiety with an ending of a
rather somber note, though it also points toward a
happy future.*

The Princess of France is one of Shakespeare's most exquisite young female creations: right royal, quick and witty, and with her ladies, filled with drollery and full of mischief. She is a good match for the young King of Navarre. The "courtship" of the Princess and her three ladies by the King and his three companions (or it could be vice versa from another angle when viewed from behind the convenient tree) is the main action of the play. The courtship antics come to full fruition when the King and his companions come to the ladies' pavilion in the guise of rough and cumbersome "Muscovites." They are unmasked by the knowing ladies, who are aware of their plot, and each gentleman makes his proper protestations and proposal of marriage to his chosen lady. The romance and hope for a quadruple wedding ceremony are cut short, however, when word arrives, quite unexpectedly, of the death of the King of France. The gaiety of the play suddenly takes on a somber and subdued mood. And while the Princess realizes she loves the King of Navarre, the duties of grieving daughter and princess must take precedence over personal wants and wishes.

PRINCESS

I thank you, gracious lords,
For all your fair endeavors; and entreat,
Out of a new-sad soul, that you vouchsafe
In your rich wisdom to excuse or hide
The liberal opposition of your spirits,
If over-boldly we have borne ourselves
In the converse of breath: your gentleness
Was guilty of it. Farewell, worthy lord!
A heavy heart bears not a nimble tongue:
Excuse me so, coming too short of thanks
For my great suit so easily obtain'd.
We received your letters full of love;
Your favours, the ambassadors of love;
And, in our maiden council, rated them
At courtship, pleasant jest and courtesy,
As bombast and as lining to the time:
But more devout than this in our respects
Have we not been; and therefore met your loves
In their own fashion, like a merriment.
No, no, my lord, your grace is perjured much,
Full of dear guiltiness; and therefore this:
If for my love, as there is no such cause,
You will do aught, this shall you do for me:
Your oath I will not trust; but go with speed
To some forlorn and naked hermitage,

Remote from all the pleasures of the world;
There stay until the twelve celestial signs
Have brought about the annual reckoning.
If this austere insociable life
Change not your offer made in heat of blood;
It frosts and fasts, hard lodging and thin weeds
Nip not the gaudy blossoms of your love,
But that it bear this trial and last love;
Then, at the expiration of the year,
Come challenge me, challenge me by these deserts,
And by this virgin palm now kissing thine,
I will be thine; and till that instant shut
My woeful self up in a mourning house,
Raining the tears of lamentation
For the remembrance of my father's death.
If this thou do deny, let our hands part,
Neither entitled in the other's heart.

A Midsummer Night's Dream
TITANIA—ACT II, SCENE 1

One of Shakespeare's ever enduring influences upon Western literature was his evolution of the world of the "faerie." It is with the creation of Oberon and Titania that the fairies in English folklore become benevolent and, with his Puck, that they become mischievous with sprightly hearts whose blessings could lead to welcomed benefits and not malevolent spirits bent upon punishment and confusion amongst mortals and humanity. In A Midsummer Night's Dream *Shakespeare created a fairy folk that humans need not fear, but a people that mere mortals wanted to see, to experience, to know; a fairy court to attend and from which humans wanted to receive blessings and attentions.*

But all is not well in the dales and mists of the fairy kingdoms. It's twin monarchs, Oberon and Titania, are at odds with one another. They are arguing over the guardianship of a young human boy, a changling, whom Oberon wants as his page, and whom Titania is determined to keep in her circle because his mother was a "votaress of [her] order," though mortal, and died giving birth to he boy. Titania has sworn to avoid Oberon's company (and his bed) until he agrees to let her keep the child. He is just as determined to capture the boy for his own retinue. The two fairy monarchs and their entourages meet unexpectedly in the forests outside of Athens on St. John's Eve—mid-summer's eve—one of the most magical nights of the year. They have come by their individual paths to witness and to bless the marriage of Theseus, Duke of Athens, to Hippolyta, Queen of the Amazons.

12

TITANIA

What, jealous Oberon! Fairies, skip hence:
I have forsworn his bed and company.
And never, since the middle summer's spring,
Met we on hill, in dale, forest or mead,
By paved fountain or by rushy brook,
Or in the beached margent of the sea,
To dance our ringlets to the whistling wind,
But with thy brawls thou hast disturb'd our sport.
Therefore the winds, piping to us in vain,
As in revenge, have suck'd up from the sea
Contagious fogs; which falling in the land
Have every pelting river made so proud
That they have overborne their continents:
The ox hath therefore stretch'd his yoke in vain,
The ploughman lost his sweat, and the green corn
Hath rotted ere his youth attain'd a beard;
The fold stands empty in the drowned field,
And crows are fatted with the murrion flock;
The nine men's morris is fill'd up with mud,
And the quaint mazes in the wanton green
For lack of tread are undistinguishable:
The human mortals want their winter here;
No night is now with hymn or carol blest:
Therefore the moon, the governess of floods,
Pale in her anger, washes all the air,

That rheumatic diseases do abound:
And through this distemperature we see
The seasons alter: hoary-headed frosts
Fall in the fresh lap of the crimson rose,
And on old Hiems' thin and icy crown
An odorous chaplet of sweet summer buds
Is, as in mockery, set: the spring, the summer,
The chilling autumn, angry winter, change
Their wonted liveries, and the mazed world,
By their increase, now knows not which is which:
And this same progeny of evils comes
From our debate, from our dissension;
We are their parents and original.
The fairy land buys not the child of me.
His mother was a votaress of my order:
And, in the spiced Indian air, by night,
Full often hath she gossip'd by my side,
And sat with me on Neptune's yellow sands,
Marking the embarked traders on the flood,
When we have laugh'd to see the sails conceive
And grow big-bellied with the wanton wind:
Which she, with pretty and with swimming gait
Following,—her womb then rich with my young
squire,—
Would imitate, and sail upon the land,
To fetch me trifles, and return again,
As from a voyage, rich with merchandise.

But she, being mortal, of that boy did die;
And for her sake do I rear up her boy,
And for her sake I will not part with him.

A Midsummer Night's Dream
HELENA—ACT I, SCENE I

"Ay, me! . . . The course of true love never did run smooth."

Helena has been wooed and has fallen in love with a fair youth of Athens named Demetrius. Demetrius, however, has passed over Helena and has now settled his intentions on Hermia; and he has gained the consent of Hermia's father to wed her. Hermia, however, has no interest in Demetrius for she is in love with another Athenean youth, Lysander, who returns her love. The more Helena loves Demetrius, the more he hates her. The more Hermia hates Demetrius, the more he dotes on her. When the Duke of Athens, Theseus, sides with Hermia's father and orders her to marry Demetrius, she and Lysander plan to elope.

Since Hermia and Helena have been close friends since childhood, the couple entrusts the news of their plan with her. Helena, while gentler than Hermia, is not altogether generous. She is in the maelstrom of unrequited love, and in this upheaval she decides to

15

tell Demetrius of the elopement. She hopes that by
helping him pursue Hermia, she will win Demetrius
back.

    The course of true love also never did run logical.

HELENA

Call you me fair? That fair again unsay.
Demetrius loves you fair. O happy fair!
Your eyes are lodestars, and your tongue's sweet air
More tuneable than lark to shepherd's ear
When wheat is green, when hawthorn buds appear.
Sickness is catching. O, were favor so,
Yours would I catch, fair Hermia, ere I go;
My ear should catch your voice, my eye your eye,
My tongue should catch your tongue's sweet melody.
Were the world mine, Demetrius being bated,
The rest I'd give to be to you translated.
O, teach me how you look, and with what art
You sway the motion of Demetrius' heart.
    [*Exit Lysander and Hermia*]
How happy some o'er other some can be!
Through Athens I am thought as fair as she.
But what of that? Demetrius thinks not so;
He will not know what all but he do know.
And as he errs, doting on Hermia's eyes,
So I, admiring of his qualities.

Things base and vile, holding no quantity,
Love can transpose to form and dignity.
Love looks not with the eyes, but with the mind,
And therefore is wing'd Cupid painted blind.
Nor hath Love's mind of any judgement taste;
Wings and no eyes, figure unheedy haste.
And therefore is Love said to be a child,
Because in choice he is so oft beguiled.
As waggish boys in game themselves forswear,
So the boy Love is perjured everywhere.
For ere Demetrius look'd on Hermia's eyne,
He hail'd down oaths that he was only mine;
And when this hail some heat from Hermia felt,
So he dissolved, and show'rs of oaths did melt.
I will go tell him of fair Hermia's flight.
Then to the wood will he tomorrow night
Pursue her; and for this intelligence
If I have thanks, it is a dear expense.
But herein mean I to enrich my pain,
To have his sight thither and back again.

A Midsummer Night's Dream
HELENA—ACT III, SCENE 2

*Midsummer's Eve—St. John's Eve—is a time for
magic and spells. In the woods outside Athens, where
Helena, Demetrius, Lysander, and Hermia are all*

*chasing after each other, the king of the fairies,
Oberon, is encamped. He has come to Athens to bless
the marriage of Theseus and Hippolyta. And being in
a generous mood, Oberon decides to grant Helena
the love of Demetrius by enchantment. He orders his
messenger, Puck, to drop the juice of a certain flower
into the eyes of Demetrius, and when the youth
awakes, he will dote on the first object he sees.
Oberon thinks this will be Helena. Puck, however,
mistakes Lysander for Demetrius, and through tried
remedy to resolve the blunder, both men begin to
pursue Helena through the wood, each professing his
undying devotion to her. She, of course, thinks she is
being mocked and ridiculed, and that all three of
them—Lysander, Demetrius, and Hermia—are co-
conspirators in this monstrous practical joke. Helena
sees it only as a means to do her emotional injury and
to deride her.*

HELENA

[*To Lysander and Demetrius*]
O spite! O hell! I see you all are bent
To set against me for your merriment.
If you were civil and knew courtesy,
You would not do me thus much injury.
Can you not hate me, as I know you do,
But you must join in souls to mock me too?

If you were men, as men you are in show,
You would not use a gentle lady so—
To vow, and swear, and superpraise my parts,
When I am sure you hate me with your hearts.
                    [*To Hermia*]
Now I perceive [you] have cojoin'd all three
To fashion this false sport, in spite of me.sa
Injurious Hermia, most ungrateful maid!
Have you conspired, have you with these contrived
To bait me with this foul derision?
Is all the counsel that we two have shared,
The sisters' vows, the hours that we have spent,
When we have chid the hasty-footed time
For parting us—O, is all forgot?
All school-days friendship, childhood innocence?
We, Hermia, like two artificial gods,
Have with our needles created both one flower,
Both on one sampler, sitting on one cushion,
Both warbling of one song, both in one key,
As if our hands, our sides, voices, and minds,
Had been incorporate. So we grew together,
Like to a double cherry, seeming parted,
But yet an union in partition;
Two lovely berries moulded on one stem;
So, with two seeming bodies, but one heart;
Two of the first, like coats in heraldry,
Due but to one and crowned with one crest.

And will you rent our ancient love asunder,
To join with men in scorning your poor friend?
It is not friendly, 'tis not maidenly.
Our sex, as well as I, may chide you for it,
Though I alone do feel the injury.
Have you not set Lysander, as in scorn,
To follow me and praise my eyes and face?
And made your other love, Demetrius,
Who even but now did spurn me with his foot,
To call me goddess, nymph, divine and rare,
Precious, celestial? Wherefore speaks he this
To her he hates? And wherefore doth Lysander
Deny your love, so rich within his soul,
And tender me, forsooth, affection,
But by your setting on, by your consent?
What though I be not so in grace as you,
So hung upon with love, so fortunate,
But miserable most, to love unloved?
This you should pity rather than despise.
Ay, do, persever, counterfeit sad looks,
Make mouths upon me when I turn my back,
Wink at each other, hold the sweet jest up.
This sport, well carried, shall be chronicled.
If you have any pity, grace, or manners,
You would not make me such an argument.
But fare ye well. 'Tis partly my own fault,
Which death, or absence, soon shall remedy.

As You Like It
ROSALIND—ACT III, SCENE 2

One of the two most famous "breeches" parts in Shakespeare is Rosalind, daughter of the banished Duke, rightful ruler of the unnamed dominions where the Forest of Arden is located. And what a heroine of a play that is pure romantic comedy is Rosalind. She is a woman who is secure in who she is, even though circumstances which surround her may cause her trouble. She bubbles with wit, and she sparkles with spirit. She dances to the melodies of life. Her heart is an overflowing fountain that washes life and love and joy onto the people surrounding her. She is as fresh and as exhilarating as a sunny, warm day after a month of gray, rainy, cold winter weather.

Rosalind has been driven from the ducal court by her usurping uncle. She has been accompanied into banishment by her cousin, Celia, and the court clown, Touchstone. They have taken refuge, as does nearly everyone in the play, in the idyllic forest of Arden. There, Rosalind dons male clothing and assumes the name Ganymede, a young shepherd, living with his sister, Aliena (Celia). Also wandering through the forest is Orlando, driven from his home by his older brother. Orlando saw Rosalind when at court and he fell in love with her at first sight. He has been meandering through the forest tacking love poems and epistles to his beloved Rosalind on numerous trees. Rosalind, of course, also loves Orlando. But since she is in the guise of a boy, she can't declare her acceptance of his attentions very well.

Rosalind overhears Orlando confess his passion for her to the melancholy Jacques, and decides to "Speak to [Orlando] like a saucy lackey and under the habit play the knave with him." In that way, Rosalind hatches a scheme of how she may keep company with Orlando without foregoing her alias.

ROSALIND

There is none of my uncle's marks upon you: he taught me how to know a man in love; in which cage of rushes I am sure you are not prisoner. A lean cheek, which you have not, a blue eye and sunken, which you have not, an unquestionable spirit, which you have not, a beard neglected, which you have not; but I pardon you for that, for simply your having in beard is a younger brother's revenue: then your hose should be ungartered, your bonet unbanded, your sleeve unbuttoned, your shoe untied and every thing about you demonstrating a careless desolation; but you are no such man; you are rather point-device in your accoutrements as loving yourself than seeming the lover of any other. But, in good sooth, are you he that hangs the verses on the trees, wherein Rosalind is so admired? Are you so much in love as your rhymes speak? Love is merely a madness, and, I tell you, deserves as well a dark house and a whip as madmen do: and the reason why they are not so punished and cured is, that the lunacy is so ordinary that the whippers are in love too. Yet I profess curing it by counsel [such a one], and in this manner. He was to imagine me his love, his mistress; and I set him every day to woo me: at which time would I, being but a moonish youth, grieve, be effeminate, changeable, longing and liking, proud, fantastical, apish, shallow, inconstant, full of tears, full of smiles, for every passion something and for no passion truly any thing, as boys and women are for the most part cattle of this colour; would now like him, now loathe him; then entertain him, then forswear him; now weep for him, then spit at him; that I drave my suitor from his mad humor of love to a living humour of madness; which was, to forswear the full stream of the world and to live in a nook merely monastic. And thus I cured him; and this way will I take upon me to wash your liver as clean as a sound sheep's heart, that there shall not be one spot of love in't.

As You Like It
ROSALIND—ACT III, SCENE 5

As You Like It *is pure comedy, with only a touch of more serious intentions making up its foundation, like all good comedic scripts.*

The spirit of As You Like It *is embodied in its heroine, Rosalind. She is as fresh and exhilarating as a sunny spring morning. Rosalind is a fountain from whose overflowing heart life, love, and joy spurt to the world and people surrounding her. She is sweet and affectionate, impulsive and voluble. And she is witty, but her wit is not that which dazzles and flashes, like, say, Beatrice's. Rosalind's wit bubbles and sparkles and dances on the air about her.*

Rosalind, the daughter of the exiled duke, has been driven from court by her usurping uncle. She has taken refuge in the Forest of Arden. She is accompanied by her cousin, Celia, and the court jester, Touchstone. To escape detection, Rosalind assumes the role of a youth named Ganymede, and Celia poses as "his" sister, Aliena. Thinking that Ganymede is really a youth, a shepherdess named Phebe conceives a silly infatuation for Ganymede/Rosalind, while spurning another shepherd, Silvius, who himself yearns for Phebe.

Rosalind, Celia, and another shepherd named Corin have come upon Phebe and Silvius, who are engaged in one of their "courtship" fracases. Phebe diverts her attention to Ganymede/Rosalind, which Rosalind refuses to accept, and she attempts in a firm, caustic attitude to send Phebe back into the willing arms of Silvius.

ROSALIND

        Who might be your mother,
That you insult, exult, and all at once,
Over the wretched? What though you have no beauty—
As, by my faith, I see no more in you
Than without candle may go dark to bed—
Must you be therefore proud and pitiless?
Why, what means this? Why do you look on me?
I see no more in you than in the ordinary
Of nature's sale-work. 'Od's my little life,
I think she means to tangle my eyes too!
No, faith, proud mistress, hope not after it.
'Tis not your inky brows, your black silk hair,
Your bugle eyeballs, nor your cheek of cream
That can entame my spirits to your worship.
You foolish shepherd, wherefore do you follow her,
Like foggy south, puffing with wind and rain?

You are a thousand times a properer man
Than she a woman. 'Tis such fools as you
That makes the world full of ill-favor'd children.
'Tis not her glass, but you, that flatters her,
And out of you she sees herself more proper
Than any of her lineaments can show her.
But, mistress, know yourself. Down on your knees,
And thank heaven, fasting, for a good man's love;
For I must tell you friendly in your ear,
Sell when you can, you are not for all markets.
Cry the man mercy; love him, take his offer.
Foul is most foul, being foul to be a scoffer.
So take her to thee, shepherd. Fare you well.
Come, sister. Shepherdess, look on him better,
And be not proud. Though all the world could see,
None could be so abused in sight as he.
Come, to our flock.

As You Like It
PHEBE—ACT III, SCENE 5

*Phebe is quite a country coquette. She is referred to
as an Arcadian beauty, and she is described as
having inky brows, black silk hair, bugle eyeballs,
and cheeks of cream. Phebe is loved by Silvius, a
young shepherd who is both humble and long-
suffering. Nothing Phebe does can repel his attention*

*nor stave off his ardor, both of which Phebe likes
when she needs them. But Phebe has spotted
Ganymede (Rosalind) and has focused her inconstant
amorous attentions on "him," much to Ganymede's
dismay. Rosalind tries immediately to squelch
Phebe's hopes and advances, but Phebe is a girl who,
once her mind is set, takes a sturdy "no" as a definite
"maybe." She also uses her wiles to keep the
shepherd she already has in her pen. She does not
like to be rejected—the attentions from a male have
probably never walked away from her before this
moment. It's quite a new and unpleasant experience
for her.*

PHEBE

Know'st thou the youth that spoke to me erewhile?
Think not I love him, though I ask for him;
'Tis but a peevish boy; yet he talks well;
But what care I for words? yet words do well
When he that speaks them pleases those that hear.
It is a pretty youth: not very pretty:
But, sure, he's proud, and yet his pride becomes him:
He'll make a proper man: the best thing in him
Is his complexion; and faster than his tongue
Did make offence his eye did heal it up.
He is not very tall; yet for his years he's tall:

His leg is but so so; and yet 'tis well:
There was a pretty redness in his lip,
A little riper and more lusty red
Than that mix'd in his cheek; 'twas just the difference
Betwixt the constant red and mingled damask.
There be some women, Silvius, had they mark'd him
In parcels as I did, would have gone near
To fall in love with him; but, for my part,
I love him not nor hate him not; and yet
I have more cause to hate him than to love him:
For what had he to do to chide at me?
He said mine eyes were black and my hair black:
And, now I am remember'd, scorn'd at me:
I marvel why I answered not again:
But that's all one; omittance is no quittance.
I'll write him a very taunting letter,
The matter's in my head and in my heart;
I will be bitter with him and passing short.
And thou shall bear it, Silvus. Go with me.

The Merry Wives of Windsor
MISTRESS QUICKLY—ACT II, SCENE 2

*The last play Shakespeare composed containing Sir
John Falstaff,* The Merry Wives of Windsor, *is a
farce centered on the antics of the middle-class from
which Shakespeare sprang. This time Mistress*

Quickly, who seems to be paired with Falstaff in the way Margaret Dumont is with Groucho Marx, is the respectable housekeeper of one Dr. Caius, a French Physician who murders the language in broken English. But Mistress Quickly has not changed her spots all that much. This Mistress Quickly, while having been given a larger part in the intrigues against Sir John, is still inclined to be as much of a bawd as ever—just as is the Mistress Quickly, hostess of the Boar's Head Tavern in Eastcheap.

Mistress Quickly is something of an emissary and go-between, a connection amongst all the intrigues that make up this play's plot. She is engaged by the foolish Slender and his ninny friends to help in his romantic pursuit of the lovely Anne Page. As a result, Mistress Quickly comes into contact with the Mistresses Ford and Page who use her as a vessel to convey their messages to the garrulous Sir John as part of their plot to entrap and humiliate him for his grandiose romantic affronts he has tendered to them. Having agreed to become part of the intrigue, Mistress Quickly comes to the Garter Inn to entice the credulous Falstaff with promissory messages from Mistress Ford and Mistress Page, co-objects of the fat knight's present amours.

MISTRESS QUICKLY

Give your worship good morrow. Shall I vouchsafe
your worship a word of two? There is one Mistress
Ford, sir:— I pray, come a little nearer this ways:—I
myself dwell with Master Doctor Caius,—I pray your
worship, come a little nearer this ways. Why, sir,
[Mistress Ford's] a good creature. Lord, Lord! your
worship's a wanton! Well, heaven forgive you and all
of us, I pray! Marry, this is the short and the long of
it; you have brought her into such a canaries as 'tis
wonderful. The best courtier of them all, when the
court lay at Windsor, could never have brought her to
such a canary. Yet there has been knights, and lords,
and gentlemen, with their coaches, I warrant you,
coach after coach, letter after letter, gift after gift;
smelling so sweetly, all musk, and so rushing, I
warrant you, in silk and gold; and in such alligant
terms; and in such wine and sugar of the best and the
fairest, that would have won any woman's heart; and,
I warrant you, they could never get an eye-wink of
her: I had myself twenty angels given me this
morning; but I defy all angels, in any such sort, as
they say, but in the way of honesty: and, I warrant
you, they could never get her so much as sip on a cup
with the proudest of them all: and yet there has been
earls, nay, which is more, pensioners; but, I warrant

you, all is one with her. Marry, she hath received your letter for which she thanks you a thousand times; and she gives you to notify that her husband will be absence from his house between ten and eleven. and then you may come and see the picture, she says, that you wot of: Master Ford, her husband, will be from home. Alas! the sweet woman leads a ill life with him: he's a very jealous man: she leads a very frampold life with him. But I have another messenger to your worship. Mistress Page hath her hearty commendations to you too: and let me tell you in your ear, she's as fartuous a civil modest wife, and one, I tell you, that will not miss you morning nor evening prayer, as any is in Windsor, whoe'er be the other; and she bade me tell your worship that her husband is seldom from home; but she hopes there will come a time. I never knew a woman so dote upon a man: surely I think you have charms, la; yes, in truth. But Mistress Page would desire you to send her your little page, of all loves; her husband has a marvelous infection to the little page; and truly Master Page is an honest man. Never a wife in Windsor leads a better life than she does: do what she will, say what she will, take all, pay all, go to bed when she list, rise when she list, all is as she will: and truly she deserves it; for if there be a kind woman in Windsor, she is one. You must send her your page;

no remedy. [Do] so then: and, look you, he may come and go between you both; and in any case have a nay-word, that you may know one another's mind, and the boy never need to understand any thing; for 'tis not good that children should know any wickedness: old folks, you know have discretion, as they say, and know the world.

The Comedy of Errors
ADRIANA—ACT II, SCENE 2

Adriana is the wife of Antipholus of Ephesus. From her first appearance in the play, she is portrayed as a suspicious and jealous wife, tending toward shrewishness. On the surface, this seems to be caused by his absences and actions and wandering eye. But the roots of her suspicions and jealousies are more deeply planted than just the fear of adultery. She is unhappy with her circumstances. She wants to know why there is an inequality between the sexes— between husband and wife: "Why should their liberty than ours be more?"

On this certain day, her husband has not appeared for dinner, and his servant, Dromio of Ephesus, tells her a strange tale of being beaten by Antipholus, who has both accused his servant of stealing gold the servant has never seen and has denied having a wife. Adriana decides it's time to confront her husband, and she goes into the marketplace to search for him. She takes her sister, Luciana, with her. The two women encounter an Antipholus and a Dromio in a public place. Each man looks exactly like her husband and servant. However, they are Antipholus of Syracuse and Dromio of Syracuse, freshly arrived in Ephesus and the twins of said husband and servant. No one knows on either side of the mirror that the other set of twins exist. Adriana thinks she has found and confronted her errant and wandering husband. Antipholus of Syracuse thinks he has encountered two madwomen— and yet, perhaps, an opportunity. Mistaken identity is the fuel which powers the engine that drives the action of this play forward.

ADRIANA

Ay, ay, Antipholus, look strange and frown.
Some other mistress hath thy sweet aspects;
I am not Adriana nor thy wife.
The time was once when thou unurged wouldst vow
That never words were music to thine ear,
That never object pleasing in thine eye,
That never touch well welcome to thy hand,
That never meat sweet-savour'd in thy taste,

Unless I spake, or look'd, or touch'd, or carv'd to
thee.
How comes it now, my husband, O, how comes it,
That thou art thus estranged from thyself?
Thyself I call it, being strange to me,
That, undividable, incorporate,
Am better than thy dear self's better part.
Ah, do not tear away thyself from me!
For know, my love, as easy mayst thou fall
A drop of water in the breaking gulf
And take unmingled thence that drop again,
Without addition or diminishing,
As take from me thyself and not me too.
How dearly would it touch thee to the quick,
Shouldst thou but hear I were licentious
And that this body, consecrate to thee,
By ruffian lust should be contaminate!
Wouldst thou not spit at me, and spurn at me,
And hurl the name of husband in my face,
And tear the stain'd skin off my harlot-brow,
And from my false hand cut the wedding-ring,
And break it with deep-divorcing vow?
I know thou canst, and therefore see thou do it.
I am possess'd with an adulterate blot;
My blood is mingled with the crime of lust;
For if we two be one and thou play false,
I do digest the poison of thy flesh,

Being strumpeted by thy contagion.
Keep then fair league and truce with thy true bed;
I live unstain'd, thou undishonored.

The Merchant of Venice
PORTIA—ACT IV, SCENE 1

Portia, heiress of Belmont, possesses beauty, wealth, and wit. She is generous, sympathetic with the less fortunate, impulsive, and ardent. She is high-spirited, intelligent, clear-sighted, noble, loyal, prompt, and decisive in action. Her sense of honor is so highly principled that she gives no hint to the lover of her choice as to which casket is the correct one to win her and her fortune—although it would mean her happiness. No wonder this girl is a prized catch, and one of the most legendary and captivating heroines in Shakespeare's canon.

Portia has secretly followed her new husband, Bassanio, back to Venice to be of what aid she can in the suit between Antonio, the merchant of Venice, and Shylock, the Jewish usurer. Portia knows that as a woman she can be of little more consequence to the trial than as moral support. But disguised as a doctor of laws (and as a man) she might be able to bring some reason to bear and influence the judgment of the ducal court.

Portia appears at the trial in the guise of Balthasar, one doctor of laws from Rome. As Balthasar, she attempts to settle the suit and save Antonio's life. At first, even in this disguise, Portia uses womanly persuasion ("The quality of mercy is not strain'd . . . ") to bring Shylock to relent on the grounds of mercy and humanity. When that approach fails to move Shylock, Portia springs the legal trap that makes her intellect greatly honored in the court. She sees a loophole in the deed of forfeiture which enables her to use the very law to which Shylock clings so rigidly to her advantage and, thus, to defeat Shylock's claim.

PORTIA

I pray you, let me look upon the bond.
          Why this bond is forfeit;
And lawfully by this the Jew may claim
A pound of flesh, to be by him cut off
Nearest the merchant's heart. Be merciful.
Take thrice thy money; bid me tear the bond.
          [No.] Why then, thus it is:
You must prepare your bosom for his knife.
For the intent and purpose of the law
Hath full relation to the penalty,
Which here appeareth due upon the bond.

Therefore lay bare your bosom.

Have by some surgeon, Shylock, on your charge,

To stop his wounds, lest he do bleed to death.

It is not so express'd, but what of that?

'Twere good you do so much for charity.

A pound of that same merchant's flesh is thine.

The court awards it, and the law doth give it.

And you must cut this flesh from off his breast.

The law allows it, and the court awards it.

Tarry a little; there is something else.

This bond doth give thee here no jot of blood;

The words expressly are "a pound of flesh."

Take then thy bond, take thou thy pound of flesh;

But, in the cutting it, if thou dost shed

One drop of Christian blood, thy lands and goods

Are, by the laws of Venice, confiscate

Unto the state of Venice.

              Thyself shalt see the act;

For, as thou urgest justice, be assured

Thou shalt have justice, more than thou desir'st.

Soft!

The Jew shall have all justice. Soft, no haste.

He shall have nothing but the penalty.

Therefore prepare thee to cut off the flesh.

Shed thou no blood, nor cut thou less nor more

But just a pound of flesh; if thou tak'st more

Or less than a just pound, be it but so much

As makes it light or heavy in the substance
Or the division of the twentieth part
Of one poor scruple, nay, if the scale do turn
But in the estimation of a hair,
Thou diest, and all thy good are confiscate.
Why doth the Jew pause? Take thy forfeiture.
            Tarry, Jew!
The law hath yet another hold on you.
It is enacted in the laws of Venice,
If it be proved against an alien
That by direct or indirect attempts
He seeks the life of any citizen,
The party 'gainst the which he doth contrive
Shall seize one half his goods; the other half
Comes to the privy coffer of the state,
And the offender's life lies in the mercy
Of the duke only, 'gainst all other voice.
In which predicament, I say, thou stand'st;
For it appears, by manifest proceeding,
That indirectly and directly too
Thou hast contrived against the very life
Of the defendant; and thou hast incurr'd
The danger formerly by me rehearsed.
Down therefore and beg mercy of the Duke.

Twelfth Night
VIOLA—ACT II, SCENE 2

*Twelfth Night is the last of Shakespeare's great
romantic comedies, and the last truly sunny comedy
he wrote. It is also one of his brightest and most
delectable. It is a play that sings with a lilt: a play
filled with music and musical references, many of
them wry comments on lovers' "melancholy" sighs. It
is a play of gentle-folk and of a gentle life.*

*Viola, the play's heroine, is one of the most
attractive women in all of Shakespeare's plays. She is
not attractive so much for her mind or her wit—she
has not the tongue nor the able quick response of her
sisters Rosalind or Beatrice, nor does she have the
ability to endure suffering stoically as does her
cousin, Hero. No, Viola is appealing for her tender
heart, her steadfast loyalty to those she loves, even at
personal cost, and for the delicacy and refinement of
her character.*

*Viola is shipwrecked and alone on the sea coast of
Illyria, a stranger in a strange land, a woman who
must survive. To do so, she assumes the guise of a
youth, "Caesario," and obtains service as a page to a
local duke, Orsino. Viola promptly falls in love with
the duke. The duke, however, is pining away for the
Countess Olivia, who is in mourning for her brother*

and is not accepting suit from anyone. Viola becomes
the love-cavalier between Orsino and Olivia. Olivia,
of course, swiftly becomes enamored with the
handsome youth, Caesario/Viola. To ensure Caesario
will return to her, Olivia sends her steward,
Malvolio, after Viola to give her back her ring, which
the youth/girl allegedly delivered from the duke (she
did not).

Malvolio has just curtly returned the ring to Viola
and has left her alone. The girl, mystified by this
event, has the sudden revelation of the awkward
situation in which she is finding herself—and the
possible consequences of the game she must continue
to play.

VIOLA

I left no ring with her. What means this lady?
Fortune forbid my outside have not charm'd her!
She made good view of me; indeed, so much,
That sure methought her eyes had lost her tongue,
For she did speak in starts distractedly.
She loves me, sure! The cunning of her passion
Invites me in this churlish messenger.
None of my lord's ring? Why, he sent her none.
I am the man. If it be so, as 'tis,
Poor lady, she were better love a dream.
Disguise, I see, thou art a wickedness.

Wherein the pregnant enemy does much.
How easy it is for the proper-false
In women's waxen hearts to set their forms!
Alas, our frailty is the cause, not we,
For such as we are made of, such we be.
How will this fadge? My master loves her dearly;
And I, poor monster, fond as much on him;
And she, mistaken, seems to dote on me.
What will become of this? As I am man,
My state is desperate for my master's love;
As I am woman—now alas the day—
What thriftless signs shall poor Olivia breathe!
O time! Thou must untangle this, not I;
It is too hard a knot for me t' untie!

All's Well That Ends Well
HELENA—ACT III, SCENE 2

Though categorized with comedies, there is little merriment in All's Well that Ends Well.

Helena, too, is a catalogue of contradictions. She possesses great amiability and an indomitable inner strength. At the same time she is both clever and self-sacrificing, both meek and high-spirited, both stead-fastly loyal and independent. She is willing to lose if necessary, but she is also quick to see a way to win what she desires. She appears to be a simple, straight-forward, and innocent girl; yet she is firm and clear-headed about the solutions to her increasingly complicated dilemmas.

Helena is in love with Bertram, the callow, young Count of Rossillion. Her love is unrequited. Bertram has never thought of her romantically, and he considers her truly beneath him because of her parentage. Unless a miracle happens, she will never marry him.

And Helena makes the necessary miracle occur. She cures the King of his illness. As a reward, the King awards her any young man at court as her husband. She chooses Bertram. He is furious, but cannot disobey the King's command. But Bertram refuses to consummate the marriage, and he sends Helena back to his mother and his estates. Once there, she's delivered a letter from him that states, "Till I have no wife, I have nothing in France." Helena has just read this letter in the presence of the Dowager Countess and the gentlemen of the court who escorted her to Rossillion. Now, she is alone. Even at this juncture of immense rejection and hurt, Helena is willing still to make excuses for Bertram, so in love with him is she. She is willing to accept the blame for his desertion and hopes only for his safety.

HELENA

"Till I have no wife, I have nothing in France."
Nothing in France, until he has no wife!
Thou shalt have none, Rossillion, none in France;
Then hast thou all again. Poor lord, is 't I
That chase thee from thy country, and expose
Those tender limbs of thine to the event
Of the none-sparing war? And is it I
That drive thee from the sportive court, where thou
Was shot at with fair eyes, to be the mark
Of smoky muskets? O you leaden messengers,
That ride upon the violent speed of fire,
Fly with false aim; move the still-peering air
That sings with piercing; do not touch my lord.
Whoever shoots at him, I set him there;
Whoever charges on his forward breast,
I am the caitiff that do hold him to 't;
And, though I kill him not, I am the cause
His death was so effected. Better 'twere
I met the ravin lion when he roar'd
With sharp constraint of hunger; better 'twere
That all the miseries which nature owes
Were mine at once. No, come thou home, Rossillion,
Whence honor but of danger wins a scar,
As oft it loses all. I will be gone.
My being here it is that holds thee hence.

Shall I stay here to do 't? No, no, although
The air of paradise did fan the house
And angels offic'd all. I will be gone,
That pitiful rumor may report my flight
To consolate thine ear. Come, night; end, day!
For with the dark, poor thief, I'll steal away.

THE TRAGEDIES

Romeo and Juilet
JULIET'S NURSE—ACT I, SCENE 3

Juliet's Nurse is a marvelous, down-to-earth woman, pragmatic about life, devoted to the Capulets, and most of all, dotes on her charge, Juliet. She is from sturdy peasant stock—probably from the country at one time. She is at turns garrulous and coarse, supportive and then deceitful, and she serves the circumstances of the times. At first she supports Juliet's secret marriage to Romeo; and once he is banished, she encourages the girl to forget that marriage as if it didn't happen and to accept the suit of Count Paris. The Nurse acts on the assumption that Romeo will never show up in Verona again. That about-face proposal reveals, more than any other, the deeply rooted base of the Nurse.

Lady Capulet has come to her daughter to inform her that Count Paris "seeks you for his love." But before Lady Capulet announces the news to Juliet, she has asked the Nurse confirmation of the girl's age. All the Nurse needs is a chink of an opening, and she is ready with a barrage of words and stories to support and illustrate her answer. The Nurse takes a

*hundred words to answer a question where only one
or two are needed.*

NURSE

Faith, I can tell her age unto an hour.
Come Lammas-eve at night shall she be fourteen.
Susan and she—God rest all Christian souls!—
Were of an age: well, Susan is with God;
She was too good for me: but, as I said,
On Lammas-eve at night shall she be fourteen;
That shall she, marry; I remember it well.
'Tis since the earthquake now eleven years;
And she was wean'd,—I never shall forget it,—
Of all the days of the year, upon that day:
For I had then laid wormwood to my dug,
Sitting in the sun under the dove-house wall;
My lord and you were then at Mantua:—
Nay, I do bear a brain:—but, as I said,
When it did taste the wormwood on the nipple
Of my dug and felt it bitter, pretty fool,
To see it tetchy and fall out with the dug!
"Shake" quoth the dove-house: 'twas no need, I trow,
To bid me trudge:
And since that time it is eleven years;
For then she could stand alone; nay, by the rood,
She could have run and waddled all about;

For even the day before, she broke her brow:
And then my husband—God be with his soul!
A' was a merry man—took up the child:
"Yea," quoth he, "dost thou fall upon thy face?
Thou wilt fall backward when thou has more wit;
Wilt thou not, Jule?" and, by my holidame,
The pretty wretch left crying and said "Ay."
To see, now, how jest shall come about!
I warrant, an I should live a thousand years,
I never should forget it: "Wilt thou not, Jule?" quoth
he;
And, pretty fool, it stinted and said "Ay."
Yes, madam: yet I cannot choose but laugh,
To think it should leave crying and say "Ay."
And yet, I warrant, it had upon its brow
A bump as big as a young cockerel's stone;
A parlous knock; and it cried bitterly:
"Yea," quoth my husband, "fall'st upon thy face?
Thou wilt fall backward when thou comest to age;
Wilt thou not, Jule?" it stinted and said "Ay."
Peace, I have done. God mark thee to his grace!
Thou wast the prettiest babe that e're I nursed:
And I might live to see thee married once,
I have my wish.

JULIET—ACT III, SCENE 2

Fourteen-year-old Juliet has been married to Romeo for approximately three hours. She is possessed by the rashness of her love for Romeo and by the daring and adventure of her recent act of defiance to her family: her secret marriage to the son of the family's enemy. She is exhilarated; she is impatient; she is anxious; she is euphoric; she is impetuous; she is edgy; she is eager; she is ardent. In short, she is a young girl in love and on the brink of what she thinks is a romantic adventure that ends only as she wants it to end: in eternal happiness and peace for both she and her Romeo.

Juliet is in the orchard of the Capulet house waiting for her Nurse to return with news from Romeo as to when he will see her. The scene has to be set out of doors because no room could contain the exuberance and excitement of this young girl. The walls would be forced open by her energy. She has to share with Nature what is most natural to her: the explosion of life that the love of Romeo causes in her.

JULIET

Gallop apace, you fiery-footed steeds,
Towards Phoebus' lodging! Such a wagoner
As Phaethon would whip you to the west,
And bring in cloudy night immediately.
Spread thy close curtain, love-performing night,
That runaways' eyes may wink, and Romeo
Leap to these arms, untalk'd of and unseen.
Lovers can see to do their amorous rites
By their own beauties; or, if love be blind,
It best agrees with night. Come, civil night,
Thou sober-suited matron, all in black,
And learn me how to lose a winning match,
Play'd for a pair of stainless maidenhoods.
Hood my unmann'd blood, bating in my cheeks,
With thy black mantle; till strange love grow bold,
Think true love acted simple modesty.
Come, night; come, Romeo; come, thou day in night;
For thou wilt lie upon the wings of night
Whiter than new snow on a raven's back.
Come, gentle night, come, loving, black-brow'd
night,
Give me my Romeo; and, when he shall die,
Take him and cut him out in little stars,
And he will make the face of heaven so fine
That all the world will be in love with night

And pay no worship to the garish sun.
O, I have bought the mansion of a love,
But not possess'd it, and, though I am sold,
Not yet enjoy'd. So tedious is this day
As is the night before some festival
To an impatient child that hath new robes
And may not wear them. O, here comes my nurse,
And she brings news; and every tongue that speaks
But Romeo's name speaks heavenly eloquence.

Romeo and Juliet
JULIET—ACT III, SCENE 2

*How quickly euphoria turns to calamity. The Nurse
has returned with the news of Romeo for Juliet, but
not the news that she expected. The Nurse tells Juliet
of Tybalt's death at Romeo's hands. At first Juliet
thinks it is Romeo who is slain, and her world
collapses. And then, when she sorts out the truth, she
reviles Romeo for killing her beloved cousin (and
now his kinsman, too). When the Nurse, in her grief,
again berates Romeo for his revenge on the death of
Mercutio, Juliet switches emotions again and
upbraids the Nurse for maligning Romeo.*

JULIET

Blister'd be thy tongue
For such a wish! He was not born to shame.
Upon his brow shame is ashamed to sit;
For 'tis a throne where honor may be crown'd
Sole monarch of the universal earth.
O, what a beast was I to chide at him!
Shall I speak ill of him that is my husband?
Ah, poor my lord, what tongue shall smooth thy name
When I, thy three-hours wife, have mangled it?
But, wherefore, villain, didst thou kill my cousin?
That villain cousin would have killed my husband.
Back, foolish tears, back to your native spring;
Your tributary drops belong to woe,
Which you, mistaking, offer up to joy.
My husband lives, that Tybalt would have slain,
And Tybalt's dead, that would have slain my husband.
All this is comfort. Wherefore weep I then?
Some word there was, worser than Tybalt's death,
That murder'd me. I would forget it fain,
But, O, it presses to my memory
Like damned guilty deeds to sinners' minds:
"Tybalt is dead, and Romeo—banished."
That 'banished,' that one word 'banished,'
Hath slain ten thousand Tybalts. Tybalt's death

Was woe enough, if it had ended there;
Or, if sour woe delights in fellowship
And needly will be rank'd with other griefs,
Why follow'd not, when she said "Tybalt's dead,"
Thy father, of thy mother, nay, or both,
Which modern lamentation might have moved?
But with the rearward following Tybalt's death,
"Romeo is banished," to speak that word,
Is father, mother, Tybalt, Romeo, Juliet,
All slain, all dead. "Romeo is banished!"
There is no end, no limit, measure, bound,
In that word's death; no words can that woe sound.
O, find him! Give this ring to my true knight,
And bid him come to take his last farewell.

Julius Caesar
PORTIA—ACT II, SCENE 1

Portia, wife of Brutus, the play's presumptive hero, is one of the only two women in Julius Caesar; *Calpurnia, Caesar's wife, is the other. Portia has but two scenes, and in the first one Shakespeare compacts the life, loves, worries, hopes, and fortitude of this noble woman.*

Brutus has been approached by Cassius and a group of conspirators to join with them in the planned assassination of Caesar. (The conspirators

need Brutus' participation to add a legitimate gloss
to their mealy plan.) Whereas before in their
marriage Brutus has always confided and consulted
with Portia, this time he keeps her at an emotional
distance, and he also keeps his own counsel. Portia
has absorbed in silence as much of this
uncharacteristic behavior of her husband as she can
bear, but now Brutus has left their bed chamber in
the middle of an unruly night to roam in the orchard.
Portia, hurt by his actions and the closure of himself
from her, confronts him.

PORTIA

Brutus, my lord! You've ungently, Brutus,
Stole from my bed. And yesternight, at supper,
You suddenly arose, and walk'd about,
Musing and sighing, with your arms across,
And when I ask'd you what the matter was,
You stared upon me with ungentle looks.
I urged you further; then you scratch'd your head,
And too impatiently stamp'd with your foot.
Yet I insisted, yet you answer'd not,
But, with and angry wafture of your hand,
Gave sign for me to leave you. So I did,
Fearing to strengthen that impatience
Which seem'd too much enkindled, and withal

Hoping it was but an effect of humor,
Which sometime hath his hour with every man.
It will not let you eat, nor talk, nor sleep,
And could it work so much on your shape
As it hath much prevail'd on your condition,
I should not know you, Brutus. Dear my lord,
Make me acquainted with your cause of grief.
Is Brutus sick? And is it physical
To walk unbraced and suck up the humors
Of the dank morning? What, is Brutus sick,
And will he steal out of his wholesome bed
To dare the vile contagion of the night,
And tempt the rheumy and unpurged air
To add unto his sickness? No, my Brutus,
You have some sick offense within your mind,
Which, by the right and virtue of my place,
I ought to know of. And, upon my knees,
I charm you, by my once-commended beauty,
By all your vows of love, and that great vow
Which did incorporate and make us one,
That you unfold to me, yourself, your half,
Why are you heavy, and what men tonight
Have had resort to you, for here have been
Some six or seven, who did hide their faces
Ever from darkness.
Within the bond of marriage, tell me, Brutus,
Is it excepted I should know no secrets

That appertain to you? Am I yourself
But, as it were, in sort of limitation,
To keep you at meals, comfort your bed,
And talk to you sometimes? Dwell I but in the
suburbs
Of your good pleasure? If it be no more,
Portia is Brutus' harlot, not his wife.

Hamlet
OPHELIA—ACT III, SCENE 1

*The Fair Ophelia! Is she noble and naive, or a pawn
and a dupe, or is she just plain stupid? That she is in
love with Hamlet there is no doubt. That Hamlet has
at least lead Ophelia to believe her love is returned
from him, there is no doubt; and it can be interpreted
from statements made by Hamlet late in the play that
his love for her was true. And in contrast to Laertes'
warning to his sister that Hamlet's station does no
allow him to give his promises freely, Gertrude's
lament over Ophelia's grave that she had hoped the
girl would have been sweet Hamlet's wife shows that
Ophelia was of rank high enough to be considered
seriously as a future queen.*

*Hamlet's most bitter words in the play are to
Ophelia. Why? Is it for the reason psychology would
tell us: that at moments of soul rendering, when a*

person is being shredded in two, there is the desire to mortify and to destroy the person one loves most? Or is it from Hamlet's awareness of the intrigues which surround him, and he is vicious to the girl simply to protect her from danger? Or does he truly believe she is another who has betrayed him? For whatever the reason, Ophelia has just experienced a biting and confounding encounter with the man she deeply loves, and with the man who, always before, had been solicitous and considerate to her. Now she is deserted, alone, and she bleeds.

OPHELIA

O, what a noble mind is here o'erthrown!
The courtier's, soldier's, scholar's, eye, tongue, sword;
The expectancy and rose of the fair state,
The glass of fashion and the mould of form,
The observed of all observers, quite, quite down!
And I, of ladies most deject and wretched,
That suck'd the honey of his music vows,
Now see that noble and most sovereign reason,
Like sweet balls jangled, out of tune and harsh;
That unmatch'd form and feature of blown youth
Blasted with ecstasy: O, woe is me,
To have seen what I have seen, see what I see!

Hamlet
QUEEN GERTRUDE—ACT IV, SCENE 7

Personal sorrows mount close upon new calamities in the troubled kingdom of Denmark. Laertes has recently returned from France to learn that his father, Polonius, was killed by Prince Hamlet, who had gotten away scot-free for doing it; that Polonius, to add insult to injury, was not buried honorably with the heraldic ceremony due his position; and, finally, he finds his sister, Ophelia, has lost her sanity.

Claudius and his queen, Gertrude, work together in their most personal and political collaboration to keep Laertes under control and to prevent him from murderous outbursts. These outbursts especially concern Gertrude because they are aimed against both her husband and her son. Just as it seems that Claudius has managed to allay Laertes, Gertrude brings the news that Ophelia has drowned. The queen gives her detailed description of the death of Ophelia in reply to Laertes' anguished "Drown'd! O, where?" This comes from his deep-rooted need to know what and where it happened, and to be taken to his sister.

The Queen's main objective is to assuage Laertes' anxieties and to keep him from renewing his murderous impulses. Her detailed description is not a ghoulish recounting, but a means to convince Laertes that Ophelia's death was an accident. Her intention is to convince Laertes that Ophelia went to her death with no terror and that she never actually realized the danger she was in.

It is interesting that the Queen's recitation is that of an observer who might, from a distance, interpret the witnessed scene in just such a manner, while one who overhears the tale might interpret the act in a completely different way—as happens later in the play.

QUEEN GERTRUDE

One woe doth tread upon another's heel,
So fast they follow. Your sister's drown'd, Laertes.
There is a willow grows askant the brook,
That shows his hoar leaves in the glassy stream;
Therewith fantastic garlands did she make
Of crow-flowers, nettles, daisies, and long purples
That liberal shepherds give a grosser name,
But our cold maids do dead men's fingers call them.
There, on the pendent boughs her cronet weeds
Clamb'ring to hang, an envious sliver broke,
When down her weedy trophies and herself
Fell in the weeping brook. Her clothes spread wide,
And, mermaid-like, awhile they bore her up,

Which time she chanted snatches of old hymns;
As one incapable of her own distress,
Or like a creature native and indued
Unto that element. But long it could not be
Till that her garments, heavy with their drink,
Pull'd the poor wretch from her melodious lay
To muddy death.
Drown'd, drown'd.

Othello
DESDEMONA—ACT I, SCENE 3

Desdemona has always been hailed as the sacrificial victim of both Othello and Iago, "a victim consecrated from the first," as one 19th century commentator wrote. But Desdemona does not know she is a victim, nor does she see herself as a potential one until near the conclusion of her story. Desdemona is, in fact, like so many of Shakespeare's women, very brave and piquantly outspoken in her innocence.

Like Juliet, Desdemona is rash in her love for Othello. In 16th century terms, it was a very grievous fault for a daughter to marry without her father's knowledge or consent. Brabantio, her father, thinks Desdemona was gulled into marriage by witchcraft, has forced Othello before the Duke of Venice at

sword's point. At Othello's request, the Duke
summons Desdemona to give testimony on Othello's
behalf—or to refute him. Desdemona, with natural
gentleness and refined grace, defies both her family
and the conventional attitude of Venice. She is,
indeed, a brave young woman.

DESDEMONA

My noble father,
I do perceive here a divided duty.
To you I am bound for life and education;
My life and education both do learn me
How to respect you. You are the lord of duty;
I am hitherto your daughter. But here's my husband,
And so much duty as my mother show'd
To you, preferring you before her father,
So much I challenge that I may profess
Due to the Moor my lord.
Most gracious Duke,
To my unfolding lend your prosperous ear,
And let me find a charter in your voice
T' assist my simpleness.
That I did love the Moor to live with him,
My downright violence and storm of fortunes
May trumpet to the world. My heart's subdued
Even to the very quality of my lord.

I saw Othello's visage in his mind,
And to his honors and valiant parts
Did my soul and fortunes consecrate.
So that, dear lords, if I be left behind,
A moth of peace, and he go to the war,
The rites for which I love him are bereft me,
And I a heavy interim shall support
By his dear absence. Let me go with him.

Othello
DESDEMONA—ACT III, SCENE 4

On the island of Cyprus, away from family and familiar friends, Desdemona is ripe for her sacrificial role in Iago's treachery toward Othello. At this point, Desdemona still views Iago as a loyal and reliable friend, though, perhaps, tactless, but dependable. This works to Iago's advantage. Everyone falls into his pocket, and no one seems the wiser to what he is doing. Iago has started his workings on Othello's trusting mind; he has assured that his wife, Emilia, will work on Desdemona to intercede with Othello on behalf of Cassio; and he has convinced Cassio that he should ask Desdemona for her help in regaining his place in both Othello's esteem and military ranks. Desdemona, who has an even more trusting soul than does Othello, is fully swept into the intrigue, as so

*many innocents are, by viewing everyone else's
motives in light of her own blameless ones.*

    *Cassio and Emilia have joined Desdemona in the
Cypriot castle, and Desdemona is assuring Cassio
that she will intervene with Othello on his behalf.*

DESDEMONA

           Alas, thrice-gentle Cassio!
My advocation is not now in tune.
My lord is not my lord; nor should I know him,
Were he in favor as in humor alter'd.
So help me every spirit sanctified,
As I have spoken for you all my best
And stood within the blank of his displeasure
For my free speech! You must awhile be patient.
What I can do I will, and more I will
Than for myself I dare. Let that suffice you.
           Something, sure, of state,
Either from Venice, or some unhatch'd practice
Made demonstrable here in Cyprus to him,
Hath puddled his clear spirit; and in such cases
Men's natures wrangle with inferior things,
Though great ones are their object. 'Tis even so;
For let our finger ache, and it endues
Our other healthful members even to a sense
Of pain. Nay, we must think men are not gods,

62

Nor of them look for such observancy
As fits the bridal. Beshrew me much, Emilia,
I was, unhandsome warrior as I am,
Arraigning his unkindness with my soul;
But now I find I had suborn'd the witness,
And he's indicted falsely.
I will go seek him. Cassio, walk here about.
If I do find him fit, I'll move your suit
And seek to effect it to my utter most.

Titus Andronicus
TAMORA—ACT III, SCENE 3

*Titus Andronicus is Shakespeare's first tragedy. He
wrote it very early in his career, and he tried to pour
a little bit of everything into it, both to gain the notice
and to please the tastes of the public, and also to
outdo his contemporaries. And this play nearly has it
all: rape and mutilation, madness, mayhem, betrayal,
murder, revenge, interracial love affairs, and a
cannibal banquet. It made dynamic theater for early
Elizabethan stage, and it was a popular play in
Shakespeare's day.*

*Tamora, queen of the Goths, is a thoroughly
wicked, vile, self-effacing woman. She is one of the
most singularly driven women created by
Shakespeare. She is the motor that drives the*

63

revenge-plot forward throughout the play. She swears vengeance on Titus after he refuses her pleas and sacrifices her eldest son to avenge his own sons' deaths in the Gothic wars. Tamora gulls the Roman Emperor, Saturnius, into marrying her while she continues her passionate love affair with the other recalcitrant and remorseless villain of the play, Aaron the Moor. Together they arrange for Tamora's remaining two sons to rape Titus' daughter, Lavina, and then cut out her tongue and cut off her hands so she can never tell the story of what happened to her. They murder Lavina's husband and arrange that two of Titus's sons are blamed and executed for the deed. And, finally, at a banquet given by Titus, before he does her in, Tamora is fed a fresh pie containing the meat of the bodies of her two sons as the main dish of the meal.

Somewhat improbably in all of this, Tamora finds time to be romantic and wax lovingly about the peaceful countryside. This lyric evocation of the countryside and "romantic" love occurs in a scene between Tamora and Aaron in a "lonely part of the forest." outside Rome. While the speech evokes the idea that Tamora does have a passion for Aaron, a sequence like this also works within the framework of the play as a rest does in a musical score. It is a short breathing space for the audience before the

*crescendo of violent blood baths which pour over
them immediately following.*

TAMORA

My lovely Aaron, wherefore look'st thou sad,
When every thing doth make a gleeful boast?
The birds chant melody on every bush,
The snake lies rolled in the cheerful sun,
The green leaves quiver with the cooling wind
And make a chequer'd shadow on the ground:
Under their sweet shade, Aaron, let us sit,
And, whilst the babbling echo mocks the hounds,
Replying shrilly to the well-tuned horns,
As if a double hunt were heard at once,
Let us sit down and mark their yelping noise;
And, after conflict such as was supposed
The wandering prince and Dido once enjoy'd,
When with the happy storm they were surprised
And curtain'd with a counsel-keeping cave,
We may, each wreathed in the other's arms,
Our pastimes done, possess a golden slumber;
Whiles hounds and horns and sweet melodious birds
Be unto us as is a nurse's song
Of lullaby to bring her babe asleep.
Ah, my sweet Moor, sweeter to me than life!

Macbeth
LADY MACBETH—ACT I, SCENE 5

Sometimes one of the hardest assignments an actor has in a play is the reading of a letter. If one aspect of acting is physicalizing emotions through words, letter reading on stage sometimes becomes an exercise in recitation without thought to the purpose other than information. Such is the case with Lady Macbeth's first appearance in the play: she is reading a letter reiterating events the audience already knows—unless it was put in to inform the latecomers. And since, too, this is the audience's introduction to Lady Macbeth, the actress has to consider seriously a number of choices about background and "backstory" knowledge before she steps into the stage lights. Is this the first time Lady Macbeth has read the letter, or it this several times later? Is Lady Macbeth surprised at what the letter reveals and is she planning spontaneously; or is this reading a search for confirmation and support of schemes already formulating? How well does Lady Macbeth know her husband? his dreams? his ambitions? Have they, on long Scottish winter nights, before the fire and over cups of grog, speculated on how the seize the crown for themselves? Contemplated murder? How to contrive an opportunity to eliminate Duncan? Or is Lady Macbeth "shooting from the hip"? All of the choices the actress implements on this first entrance of the Lady will direct the growth and path of the role to the heart rendering sleepwalking scene.

LADY MACBETH

[*Enter LADY MACBETH, reading a letter*]
'They met me in the day of success; and I have learned by the perfectest report, they have more in them than mortal knowledge. When I burned in desire to question them further, they made themselves air, into which they vanished. Whiles
I stood rapt in the wonder of it, came missives from the king, who all-hailed me "Thane of Cawdor"; by which title, before, the weird sisters saluted me, and referred me to the coming of time, with "Hail, king that shalt be!"
This I have thought good to deliver thee, my dearest partner of greatness, that thou mightst not lose the dues of rejoicing, by being ignorant of what greatness is promised thee. Lay it to thy heart, and farewell.'
Glamis thou art, and Cawdor; and shall be
What thou art promised: yet I do fear thy nature;
It is too full o' the milk of human kindness
To catch the nearest way: thou wouldst be great;

Art not without ambition, but without
The illness should attend it; what thou wouldst
highly,
That wouldst thou holily; wouldst not play false,
And yet wouldst wrongly win: thou'ldst have, great
Glamis,
That which cries 'Thus thou must do, if thou have it;
And that which rather thou doest fear to do
Than wishest should be undone.' Hie thee hither,
That I may pour my spirits in thine ear;
And chastise with the valour of my tongue
All that impedes thee from the golden round,
Which fate and metaphysical aid doth seem
To have crown'd withal.

King Lear
GONERIL—ACT I, SCENE 3

*"How sharper than a serpent's tooth it is/To have a
thankless child!" King Lear directs this famous pro-
nouncement to his daughter, Goneril. Even though
Lear is a foolish old man, who gives away all he has,
and then expects gratitude, in this instance he does
give an accurate insight into Goneril. Goneril is a
formidable gorgon with a heart of stone who will an-
nihilate anyone or anything that is an obstacle in her
path. There is not much good that can be said about*

the woman, if any: she betrays her father, cuckholds
her husband, poisons her collaborating sister, and
conspires to the murders of her father and youngest
sister (and probably would have murdered her own
husband had she not committed suicide). If single-
will and determination on a direct course are counted
as virtues, then Goneril's virtues have been
catalogued.

Goneril unfurls her true colors early in the play.
Once she gets control of half of the kingdom, she
wastes no time in letting everyone else know who is in
charge. King Lear has barely retired from the throne
before Goneril wants to set him down from the head
table to "below the salt." She is going over the
situation in her palace with her steward, Oswald.

GONERIL

Did my father strike my gentleman for chiding of his
fool?
By day and night he wrongs me; every hour
He flashes into one gross crime or other,
That sets us all at odds: I'll not endure it:
His knights grow riotous, and himself upbraids us
On every trifle. When he returns from hunting,
I will not speak to him; say I am sick:
If you come slack of former services,

You shall do well: the fault of it I'll answer.
Put on what weary negligence you please,
You and your fellows; I'ld have it come to question:
If he dislike it, let him to our sister,
Whose mind and mine, I know, in that are one,
Not to be over-ruled. Idle old man,
That still would manage those authorities
That he hath given away! Now, by my life,
Old fools are babes again; and must be used
With checks and flatteries,—when they are seen abused.
Remember what I tell you.
And let his knights have colder looks among you;
What grows of it, no matter; advise your fellows so:
I would breed from hence occasions, and I shall,
That I may speak: I'll write straight to my sister,
To hold my very course. Prepare for dinner.

[*Exit*]

King Lear
CORDELIA—ACT IV, SCENE 7

Juliet, Ophelia, Cordelia. This trio of heroines seem to spark the imaginations and ambitions of more young actresses than any of the other female roles from the tragedies. The mistake many young players make, however, in portraying these women is that they mistake Cordelia's tenderness and care for passivity and weakness. But Cordelia is a very strong character—a strength derived from her honesty. She is one of these people whose real feeling are too deep for words. Unfortunately, early in her story, glib words are what are desired and will carry the day.

After being disowned by her father, King Lear, Cordelia is married—without dowry—to the King of France and becomes that country's queen. Cordelia is a woman who solicits great devotion from the men around her: the Duke of Gloucester and his son, Edgar; the disgraced Earl of Kent, never waivers from his belief in her; and her husband creates an invasion force to accompany her back to Britain to save her father. And Cordelia, of course, epitomizes filial loyalty and love: through all her troubles she never slides from her love for her father.

The mad King Lear has been found by members of Cordelia's invasion force in the fields near Dover and they have brought him to the French camp, after a chase to catch him. Lear now sleeps, and Cordelia, the doctors, and the still disguised Kent are in attendance awaiting his revival with the hope that when he awakes he will have regained his wits. Cordelia verbalizes her emotions about the circumstances of her fallen father in a most intimate and private of moments.

71

CORDELIA

O you kind gods,
Cure this great breach in his abused nature!
The untuned and jarring senses, O, wind up
Of this child-changed father!
O my dear father! Restoration hang
Thy medicine on my lips; and let this kiss
Repair those violent harms that my two sisters
Have in thy reverence made!
Had you not been their father, these white flakes
Had challenged pity of them. Was this a face
To be opposed against the warring winds?
To stand against the deep dread-bolted thunder?
In the most terrible and nimble stroke
Of quick, cross lightning? to watch—poor perdu!—
With this thin helm? Mine enemy's dog,
Thought he had bit me, should have stood that night
Against my fire; and wast thou fain, poor father,
To hovel thee with swine, and rogues forlorn,
In short and musty straw? Alack, alack!
'Tis wonder that thy life and wits at once
Had not concluded all. He wakes!
How does my royal lord? How fares your majesty?
            O, look upon me, sir,
And hold your hands in benediction o'er me.

Antony and Cleopatra
CLEOPATRA—ACT I, SCENE 3

Shakespeare was writing about co-dependency long before it became fashionable jargon to toss about. Historically, one of the most infamous co-dependent couples was Antony and Cleopatra. They lost friends, reputations, and empires because they could not keep apart. Of the late tragedies, Antony and Cleopatra *is the only one that is a love tragedy—or rather the downfall of the principals is brought about by unbridled passion for each other. Cleopatra bedazzled Antony's faculties, bewitched his fancy, and bewildered his judgment. She was for Antony the kind of enchantment from which his rational senses wanted to rebel but could not escape. At turns Cleopatra used all of her wit and wiles, allurements, and vivacious imagination to play the sorceress to hold Antony—object of her passion. Against such caprices and voluptuousness, Antony didn't stand a chance, for he was the most pathetic of victims: the brave soldier who collaborated willingly with his enemy to bring about his own defeat.*

But for all of her accomplishments, fascinations, and graces, Cleopatra was, as all co-dependents seem to be, insecure in her control. She always lived in fear of losing Antony unless he was within eye-

sight and hand's reach. Business and the necessity of
ruling one-third of a great part of the known world
has called Antony back to Rome. Cleopatra, who is
no stranger to the calls of power nor to Rome, is
desperate for Antony not to leave Alexandria—and
all the reasons are personal, nothing of State. If
passion and pleading will not stay him, perhaps petu-
lance and childish conniving will.

CLEOPATRA

Pray you, stand farther from me.
I know, by that same eye, there's some good news.
What says the married woman? You may go:
Would she had never given you leave to come!
Let her not say 'tis I that keep you here:
I have no power upon you; hers you are
          O, never was there queen
So mightily betray'd! yet at the first
I saw the treasons planted.
Why should I think that you can be mine and true,
Though you in swearing shake the throned gods,
Who have been false to Fulvia? Riotous madness,
To be entangled with those mouth-made vows,
Which break themselves in swearing!
Nay, pray you, seek no colour for your going,
But bid farewell, and go: when you sued staying,

Then was the time for words: no going then;
Eternity was in our lips and eyes,
Bliss in our brows' bent; none our parts so poor,
But was a race of heaven: they are so still,
Or thou, the greatest soldier of the world,
Art turned the greatest liar.
I would I had thy inches; thou shouldst know
There were a heart in Egypt.

Antony and Cleopatra
CLEOPATRA—ACT I, SCENE 5

Antony has been away from Alexandria for some time, but Cleopatra's thoughts are never far from him. Strangely enough, with all of her insecurity, at this point she seems confident of her control over her lover, and she doesn't seem too concerned with what Antony may be doing with whom. And to Antony's credit in their relationship, Cleopatra finds life less than scintillating with him gone. Here, she is in her palace at Alexandria, surrounded by her attendants, Charmian, Iras, and the eunuch, Mardian, fully engrossed in her favorite occupation, more time consuming than even that of a ruling monarch: speculating about Antony.

CLEOPATRA

O Charmian,
Where think'st thou he is now? Stands he, or sits he?
Or does he walk? or is he on his horse?
O happy horse, to bear the weight of Antony!
Do bravely, horse! for wot'st thou whom thou
movest?
The demi-Atlas of this earth, the arm
And burgonet of men. He's speaking now,
Or murmuring 'Where's my serpent of old Nile?'
For so he calls me: now I feed myself
With most delicious poison. Think on me,
That am with Phoebus' amorous pinches black,
And wrinkled deep in time? Broad-fronted Caesar,
When thou wast here above the ground, I was
A morsel for a monarch: and great Pompey
Would stand and make his eyes grow in my brow;
There would he anchor his aspect and die
With looking on his life.

THE ROMANCES

Pericles
DIONYZA—ACT IV, SCENE 1

Dionyza is the wife to Cleon, the governor of the City of Tarsus. Early in his adventures, Pericles brings shiploads of relief goods to the suffering city, and he earns the gratitude of Cleon and Dionyza for his charity. Later, when Pericles believes his wife has died in childbirth aboard ship and has been buried at sea, he fosters his baby daughter, Marina, onto Cleon and Dionyza. He charges that they raise the baby with "princely training, that she may be/Manner'd as she born."

Marina is raised side by side with Dionyza's own daughter, Philoten. Both girls blossom, but Marina's blossoms are brighter and sweeter. While this doesn't seem to bother Philoten, it causes "rare envy" in Dionyza, who feels the virtues of her own daughter are being obscured by the abilities and traits of Marina. Dionyza decides, therefore, that the only way for Philoten to "stand peerless" against Marina is to have Marina murdered.

At this moment, Dionyza is walking along the open space near the seashore with her servant, Leonine, whom she has paid to become a murderer.

Dionyza gives him final encouragement on how safe it is to kill Marina without being detected and warns him not to let his conscience get in his way. Propitiously, Marina, who has been out picking flowers, crosses their path and gives Dionyza and Leonine their opportunity immediately.

DIONYZA

[*To Leonine*]
Thy oath remember; thou has sworn to do 't:
'Tis but a blow, which never shall be known.
Thou canst not do a thing in the world so soon,
To yield thee so much profit. Let not conscience,
Which is but cold, inflaming love i' thy bosom,
Inflame too nicely; nor let pity, which
Even women have cast off, melt thee, but be
A soldier to thy purpose.
Here she comes weeping for her nurse's death. Thou
art resolved? . . .
    [*Enter Marina, with a basket of flowers*]
How now, Marina! Why do you keep alone?
How chance my daughter is not with you? Do not
Consume your blood with sorrowing; you have
A nurse of me. Lord, how your favor's changed
With this unprofitable woe!
Come, give me your flowers, ere the sea mar it.

Walk with Leonine; the air is quick there,
And it pierces and sharpens the stomach. Come,
Leonine, take her by the arm, walk with her.
                    Come, come;
I love the King your father, and yourself,
With more than foreign heart. We every day
Expect him here. When he shall come and find
Our paragon to all reports thus blasted,
He will repent the breadth of his great voyage,
Blame both my lord and me that we have taken
No care to your best courses. Go, I pray you,
Walk, and be cheerful once again. Reserve
That excellent complexion, which did steal
The eyes of young and old. Care not for me;
I can go home alone.
Come, come, I know 'tis good for you.
Walk half an hour, Leonine, at the least.
Remember what I have said. [*Exit*]

Pericles
MARINA—ACT V, SCENE 1

Pericles *was an extremely popular and successful
play in Shakespeare's theater, which is an interesting
piece of information when one considers how
unsatisfactory is the text of the play that has come
down to us.* Pericles *is an "adventurous" play, not*

79

only in its chronicle of the hero's escapades and trials, but also in the manner in which Shakespeare wrote it. "Experimental" is the operative word.

All of the adventures in the play are painful ones. Marina has been born at sea, her mother thought to have died in child-birth, and the coffin containing the body tossed overboard into the sea. Marina is raised at Pericles' behest by foster parents, the governor of Tarsus and his wife, Dionyza. Marina outshines her foster sister, so Dionyza plots to have Marina murdered. But Marina is "rescued" from the murder by pirates who sell her into a brothel in Mytilene. She manages to escape the brothel and "chances/Into an honest house," where her reputation as a superlative entertainer and a maid of virtue blossoms. Finally, she is reunited with her father through incredulous circumstances when she is called upon, aboard ship, to cure Pericles and induce the grieving Pericles to speak for the first time in over three months. Pericles has been committing slow suicide by silence and starvation and isolation driven by grief over the "deaths" of his wife and daughter.

This is the moment in which Marina reveals herself to her father, who, of course, does not recognize her. Marina is completely ingenuous and guileless, telling her story with all simplicity of truth. (She has, by the way, just finished singing a lyrical ditty that

*has captured Pericles' attention and moved him to
speak for the first time—to anyone—in three months.
Marina embodies grace and enchantment, if nothing
else.)*

MARINA

I am a maid,
My lord, that ne'er before invited eyes,
But have been gazed on like a comet: she speaks,
My lord, that, may be, hath endured a grief
Might equal yours, if both were justly weigh'd.
Through wayward fortune did malign my state,
My derivation was from ancestors
Who stood equivalent with mighty kings:
But time hath rooted out my parentage,
And to the world and awkward casualties
Bound me in servitude. [*Aside*] I will desist:
But there is something glows upon my cheek,
And whispers in mine ear "Go not till he speak.'
I said, my lord, if you did know my parentage,
You would not do me violence.
If I should tell my history, it would seem
Like lies disdain'd in the reporting.
My name is Marina.
The name
Was given me by one that had some power,

My father, and a king. Call'd Marina
For I was born at sea.
My mother was the daughter of a king;
Who died the minute I was born,
As my good nurse Lychorida hath oft
Deliver'd weeping.
The king my father did in Tarsus leave me;
Till cruel Cleon, with his wicked wife,
Did seek to murder me: and having woo'd
A villain to attempt it, who having drawn to do't,
A crew of pirates came and rescued me;
Brought me to Mytilene. But, good sir,
Whither will you have me? Why do you weep?
It may be,
You think me an imposter: no good faith;
I am the daughter of King Pericles,
If good King Pericles be.

Cymbeline
THE QUEEN—ACT I, SCENE 5

Cymbeline's Queen could serve as the mentor for Cinderella's grasping stepmother or the wicked queen in Snow White. *Those two infamous, better-known ladies are, in fact, pale imitations of this Queen.*

Cymbeline *is an odd play. It is a mixture of romance and folklore, tragicomedy, melodrama, heroic epic, morality; and an exploration of loyalty and devotion, betrayal and deceit, truth triumphant, and love's power to forgive. It is an experimental play, more ponderous than inspired, and like so many trial experiments into untravelled realms, one that never quite makes up its mind what kind of play it wants to be. Perhaps it is kindest to say that it's a notebook of ideas, some of which are brought to fulfillment in the two masterpieces that followed it:* The Winter's Tale and The Tempest.

The Queen is at least Cymbeline's second wife and she has complete ascendancy over him. By his first wife, Cymbeline had two sons and a daughter. The two sons are thought long dead, so his daughter, Imogen, is the heir presumptive to the kingdom. The queen wants her son by a previous marriage, who is an oaf of the first rank, to succeed to the throne. To do that, however, Cloton (her son), needs to marry Imogen. Imogen not only spurns Cloton, but she also marries Posthumus Leonatius against her father's wishes.

The Queen hates Imogen for rejecting Cloton. While pretending to support Imogen, she goads Cymbeline to further punishment for the couple. The Queen is crafty, able, and totally unscrupulous.

Just a moment before, the Queen has received
from a compromised doctor, a casket of poisons
which she intends to deliver to Imogen. The Queen
cannot appear to be involved in Imogen's murder,
and she knows it. To this end, she has sent for
Pisanio, servant to Posthumus and loyal to Imogen.
She intends him to be the unknowing messenger of
Imogen's death.

QUEEN

[*Enter Pisanio*]
[*Aside*] Here comes a flattering rascal; upon him
Will I first work. He's for his master,
And enemy to my son. How now, Pisanio!
            Hark thee, a word.
Weeps she still, say'st thou? Dost thou think in time
She will not quench and let instructions enter
Where folly now possesses? Do thou work.
When thou shalt bring me word she loves my son,
I'll tell thee on the instant thou art then
As great as is thy master; greater, for
His fortunes all lie speechless and his name
Is at last gasp. Return he cannot, nor
Continue where he is. To shift his being
Is to exchange one misery with another,
And every day that comes comes to decay

A day's work in him. What shalt thou expect
To be depender on a thing that leans,
Who cannot be new built, nor has no friends,
So much as but to prop him?
[*The Queen drops the box: Pisanio takes it up*]
Thou tak'st up
Thou know'st not what; but take it for thy labor.
It is a thing I made, which hath the King
Five times redeem'd from death. I do not know
What is more cordial. Nay, I prithee, take it;
It is an earnest of a farther good
That I mean to thee. Tell thy mistress how
The case stands with her; do 't as from thyself.
Think what a chance thou changest on, but think
Thou hast thy mistress still—to boot, my son,
Who shall take notice of thee. I'll move the king
To any shape of thy preferment such
As thou 'lt desire; and then myself, I chiefly,
That set thee on to this desert, am bound
To load thy merit richly. Fare thee well, Pisanio;
Think on my words. [*Exit Pisanio*]
A sly and constant knave,
Not to be shaked; the agent for his master
And the remembrancer of her to hold
The hand-fast to her lord. I have given him that
Which, if he take, shall quite unpeople her
Of liegers for her sweet, and which she after,

Except she bend her humor, shall be assured
To taste of too.

Cymbeline
IMOGEN—ACT III, SCENE 2

*Imogen is the only daughter and last surviving child
of Cymbeline, a king of ancient Britain. She is also a
much put- upon lady, and through it all she remains
gentle, beautiful, steadfast, and, of course, innocent.
Throughout her trials, she retains her fortitude and
her grace, and, in the end, she blossoms with
magnanimity toward all. Imogene is also a young
woman with feelings and ideas of her own. Among
those ideas is that she should be allowed to follow
her heart and be able to marry whom she chooses for
love and not for reasons of state, business, or
practicality to benefit others in her family. Imogen
marries a "worthy, but poor gentleman" who is not
of her class, and by doing so incurs the wrath of her
father.*

*The King exiles Posthumus, and to his mind the
marriage is ended. Imogen, however, does not accept
it, and in far-off Rome, neither does Posthumus. So
sure is Posthumus of his lady's fidelity that he makes
an absurd bet with a new acquaintance, an Italian
named Iachimo. Iachimo bets Posthumus that he can*

bed the virtuous Imogen. (Iachimo is a cad and scoundrel who is worthy of mention in the same breath as some of Shakespeare's other unscrupulous opportunists—Italian or otherwise.)

Imogen of course spurns Iachimo. But Iachimo gains access to Imogen's bedchamber through a "trunk trick." Back in Rome, Iachimo presents Posthumus with his "proof" of his successful seduction: a bracelet he has stolen off the arm of the sleeping Imogen, plus a description of her chamber, as well as knowledge of a certain part of her hidden anatomy. Posthumus has no reason to doubt Iachimo's veracity and Imogen's infidelity.

Posthumus' pride is wounded to oceanic depths. He is betrayed and wants revenge. To this end, he writes two letters: an obsequious one to Imogen to lure her from the palace and to meet him clandestinely at Milford-Haven in Wales. The second letter is to the loyal Pisanio. This letter makes the accusation of adultery and orders Pisanio to kill Imogen once they arrive at Milford-Haven.

Imogen has just received the letter intended for her from her sorely missed Posthumus. Here is a young bride and wife whose deepest wish is about to be fulfilled.

IMOGEN

[*Reads*] "Justice, and your father's wrath, should he
take me in his dominion, could not be so cruel to me,
as you, O the dearest of creatures, would even renew
me with your eyes. Take notice that I am in Cambria,
at Milford-Haven. What your own love will out of
this advise you, follow. So he wishes you all happi-
ness that remains loyal to his vow, and your
increasing in love. Leonatus Posthumus."
O, for a horse with wings! Hear'st thou Pisanio?
He is at Milford-Haven. Read, and tell me
How far 'tis thither. If one of mean affairs
May plot it in a week, why may not I
Glide thither in a day? Then, true Pisanio,
Who long'st, like me, to see thy lord; who long'st—
O, let me bate—but not like me, yet long'st,
But in a fainter kind—O, not like me,
For mine's beyond beyond, say, and speak thick—
Love's counselor should fill the bores of hearing,
To the smothering of the sense—how far it is
To this same blessed Milford. And by the way,
Tell me how Wales was made so happy as
To inherit such a haven. But first of all,
How we may steal from hence, and for the gap
That we shall make in time from our hence-going
And our return, to excuse. But first, how get hence?

Why should excuse be born or ere begot?
We'll talk of that hereafter. Prithee, speak,
How many score of miles may we well rid
'Twixt hour and hour?
Go bid my woman feign a sickness, say
She'll home to her father; and provide me presently
A riding-suit, no costlier than would fit
A franklin's housewife.
I see before me, man. Nor here, nor here,
Nor what ensues, but have a fog in them,
That I cannot look through. Away, I prithee!
Do as I bid thee. There's no more to say.
Accessible is none but Milford way.

Cymbeline
IMOGEN—ACT III, SCENE 4

*Two scenes later in the play, Imogen and Pisanio ar-
rive at Milford-Haven. Pisanio knows that his master
is wrong and that his mistress is innocent of any
wrongdoing. He will not murder the girl, and he
shows Imogen the letter Posthumus sent him and the
real reason for their journey to Wales.*

*The contrast between Imogen's emotional reac-
tions to this second letter and her reactions to the
first help define the complexity and breadth of
emotional range and traumatic situations which*

Imogen traverses throughout the play. It is in such ex-tremes that Shakespeare creates a character that for an actress is both striking and interesting: challenge to be both bold and human at the same time.

IMOGEN

[*Reads*] "Thy mistress, Pisanio, hath played the strumpet in my bed; the testimonies whereof lie bleeding in me. I speak not out of weak surmises, but from proof as strong as my grief and as certain as I expect my revenge. That part thou, Pisanio, must act for me, if thy faith be not tainted with the breach of hers. Let thine own hands take away her life. I shall give thee opportunity at Milford-Haven—he hath my letter for the purpose—where, if thou fear to strike and to make me certain it is done, thou art the pandar to her dishonor and equally to me disloyal."
False this to bed! What is it to be false?
To lie in watch there and to think on him?
To weep 'twixt clock and clock? If sleep charge nature,
To break it with a fearful dream of him
And cry myself awake? That's false to 's bed, is it?
I false! Thy conscience witness! Iachimo,
Thou didst accuse him of incontinency;
Thou then look'dst like a villain; now methinks

Thy favor's good enough. Some jay of Italy,
Whose mother was her painting, hath betray'd him:
Poor I am stale, a garment out of fashion,
And, for I am richer than to hang by the walls,
I must be ripp'd. To pieces with me! O,
Men's vows are women's traitors! All good seeming,
By thy revolt, O husband, shall be thought
Put on for villainy; not born where 't grows,
But worn a bait for ladies.
True honest men being heard, like false Aeneas,
Were in his time thought false, and Sinon's weeping
Did scandal many a holy tear, took pity
From most true wretchedness. So thou, Posthumus,
Wilt lay the leaven on all proper men;
Goodly and gallant shall be false and perjured
From thy great fail. Come, fellow, be thou honest;
Do thou thy master's bidding. When thou see'st him,
A little witness my obedience. Look!
I draw the sword myself. Take it, and hit
The innocent mansion of my love, my heart.
Fear not; 'tis empty of all things but grief.
Thy master is not there, who was indeed
The riches of it. Do his bidding; strike.
Thou mayst be valiant in a better cause,
But now thou seem'st a coward.

        Why, I must die;
And if I do not by thy hand, thou art

No servant of thy master's. Against self-slaughter
There is prohibition so divine
That cravens my weak hand. Come, here's my heart.
Something's afore 't. Soft, soft! We'll no defense;
Obedient as the scabbard. What is here?
The scriptures of the loyal Leonatus,
All turn'd to heresy? Away, away,
Corrupters of my faith! You shall no more
Be stomachers to my heart. Thus may poor fools
Believe false teachers. Though those that are betray'd
Do feel the treason sharply, yet the traitor
Stands in worse case of woe.
And thou, Posthumus, thou that didst set up
My disobedience 'gainst the King my father
And make me put into contempt the suits
Of princely fellows, shalt hereafter find
It is no act of common passage, but
A strain of rareness: and I grieve myself
To think, when thou shalt be disedged by her
That now thou tirest on, how thy memory
Will then be pang'd by me. Prithee, dispatch.
The lamb entreats the butcher.

The Tempest
MIRANDA—ACT I, SCENE 2

*Miranda has experienced more than once in her iso-
lated life the fury of her angry, magician father,
Prospero. She has seen the results of his temper when
his wrath and fury have found expression in his "so
potent art." Miranda's knowledge of men and of
other worlds is, of course, lacking, but she is not
lacking in the natural milk of human kindness and the
concern for the welfare of others when witnessing
their torments from a safe distance. From somewhere
on the island, Miranda has seen the "tempest" roar
up from the offshore and clutch at the vessel which
contained her (unknown) uncle, the King of Naples,
Ferdinand, and all the rest. She was terrified at the
power of the storm, but she was also wise enough to
realize, since the tempest storm did not disturb the
enchanted isle that is her home, that her father and
his magic may have something to do with it—if not totally responsible for it. Miranda is a girl of fifteen,
and just becoming absorbed and concerned with life.
And she is full of the worries one has at that age,
about the inequities of the world—and the aches of
idealism to do something about them.*

MIRANDA

If by your art, my dearest father, you have
Put the wild waters in this roar, allay them.
The sky, it seems, would pour down stinking pitch,
But that the sea, mounting to the welkin's cheek,
Dashes the fire out. O, I have suffer'd
With those that I saw suffer: a brave vessel,
Who had, no doubt, some noble creature in her,
Dash'd all to pieces. O, the cry did knock
Against my heart. Poor souls, they perish'd.
Had I been any god of power, I would
Have sunk the sea within the earth or ere
It should the good ship so have swallow'd and
The fraughting souls within her.

The Tempest
MIRANDA—ACT III, SCENE 1

*Miranda was only three or four years old when she
was castaway on a strange, enchanted, uncharted island with her father. For twelve years she has had no
human contact save for her father, the austere
sorcerer Prospero, and the deformed, savage
inhabitant of the island, Caliban, who is her father's
slave. Prospero has been her only teacher and her*

only source of society. Her views have tended to reflect his until this one fateful day when she experiences a "brave new world." A shipload of men are tossed ashore by a violent sea tempest—all engineered by Prospero and his magic.

The first human Miranda sees since she was a child too young to remember them is the young prince of Naples, Ferdinand. And, as in all fairy tales controlled by magic, it is love at first sight between them. But Prospero has other plans "lest too light winning/Make the prize light." He orders Miranda not to speak to the young stranger, and he causes Ferdinand to labor in his service. Love, however, is too strong for Miranda to obey her father. She knows her father's habits—she knows when he will be otherwise occupied—and she waits for that opportunity to speak to Ferdinand. Being "unconventional" (by the rules of another's society), Miranda does not hesitate to say openly what she thinks or feels to Ferdinand.

MIRANDA

Alas, now, pray you,
Work not so hard. I would the lightning had
Burnt up those logs you are enjoin'd to pile!
Pray, set it down and rest you. When this burns,

'Twill weep for having wearied you. My father
Is hard at study; pray now, rest yourself.
He's safe for these three hours. If you'll sit down,
I'll bear your logs the while. Pray, give me that.
I'll carry it to the pile. It would become me
As well as it does you; and I should do it
With much more ease, for my good will is to it,
And yours it is against. You look wearily.
                    I do not know
One of my sex; no woman's face remember,
Save, from my glass, mine own. Nor have I seen
More that I may call men than you, good friend,
And my dear father. How features are abroad,
I am skilless of; but, by my modesty,
The jewel in my dower, I would not wish
Any companion in the world but you,
Nor can imagination form a shape,
Besides yourself, to like of. But I prattle
Something too wildly, and my father's precepts
I therein do forget. Do you love me?
                    I am a fool
To weep at what I am glad of. [I weep]
At mine unworthiness, that dare not offer
What I desire to give, and much less take
What I shall die to want. But this is trifling,
And all the more it seeks to hide itself,
The bigger bulk it shows. Hence, bashful cunning,

And prompt me, plain and holy innocence!
I am your wife, if you will marry me;
If not, I'll die your maid. To be your fellow
You may deny me, but I'll be your servant,
Whether you will or no. My husband, then?
[My hand,] with my heart in 't. And now farewell
Till half an hour hence.

Troilus and Cressida
CRESSIDA—ACT III, SCENE 2

*The legend of Troilus and Cressida was well known
to the Elizabethans, due in part to one of the sources
of the play, Chaucer's poem* Troilus and Criseyde.
*Elizabethans also had an affinity for the Trojans be-
cause one branch of their history held that England
was also founded by a group of refugee Trojans
escaping from the nasty Greeks after the fall of Troy.
But in all of these stories and legends, Cressida does
not come out with shimmering character references.
Cressida has passed into synonymous meaning of
fickleness and falsehood.*

*Cressida is the daughter of Calchas, a Trojan
priest, who has deserted Troy and joined with the
Greeks, while his daughter has remained with the
city. Troilus is one of the many sons of that over-
productive king, Priam. Troilus falls in love with*

Cressida, passionately and obsessively and honestly.
Cressida, unfortunately, is one of these women who,
if she is "not near the man she loves, loves the man
she is near." Cressida is beautiful and witty; she is
good company; she is also passionate and coquettish,
so, therefore, she is ardent and inconstant rather that
affectionate and steady. She is also a pawn of the
war. She is exchanged, at the request of her father,
for the Trojan commander Antenor, and she is sent to
the Greek camp. Once there, she forgets Troilus and
takes up with a Greek prince, Diomedes.

After the longest time of playing go-between and
match-maker, Cressida's uncle, Pandarus, has finally
arranged a successful, private assignation between
the two young people in the orchard of his home.
While Pandarus has been ever busy taking
impressions and messages back and forth between
them, this is the first extended, secluded meeting
between Troilus and Cressida. Both of them know
exactly what they want from this encounter and how
they want it to end, even though Pandarus hovers
about, solicitous and unsure.

CRESSIDA

Well, uncle, what folly I commit, I dedicate to you.
Boldness comes to me now, and brings me heart.

Prince Troilus, I have loved you night and day
For many weary months.
Hard to seem won: but I was won, my lord,
With the first glance that ever—pardon me—
If I confess much, you will play the tyrant.
I love you now; but not, till now, so much
But I might master it: in faith, I lie;
My thoughts were like unbridled children, grown
Too headstrong for their mother. See, we fools!
Why have I blabb'd? who shall be true to us,
When we are so unsecret to ourselves?
But, though I loved you well, I woo'd you not:
And yet, good faith, I wish'd myself a man,
Or that we women had men's privilege
Of speaking first. Sweet, bid me hold my tongue,
For in this rapture I shall surely speak
The thing I shall repent. See, see, your silence,
Cunning in dumbness, from my weakness draws
My very soul of counsel! stop my mouth.
My lord, I do beseech you, pardon me;
"Twas not my purpose, thus to beg and kiss:
I am ashamed. O heavens! what have I done?
For this time will I take leave, my lord.

All's Well that Ends Well
HELENA—ACT I, SCENE 1

Helena is the daughter of an accomplished physician, and she has learned his art. She is of the gentry, not the nobility, and she also has fallen in love with the young and callow Count Bertram. It is a love that is not returned. On the surface, Helena appears to be a straight-forward, innocent, and simple girl; but she possesses an indomitable inner spirit and inner strength. She seems always to be clear-headed about the solutions to the increasingly complicated dilemmas she encounters.

The first dilemma Helena faces is how to get Bertram to notice her, romantically, and then how to win him. Helena has just bid an empty farewell to Bertram, who has been summoned to the King's court, and she has just repelled the advances of Bertram's soldier companion, the braggadocio, Parolles. After these back-to-back incidents, Helena realizes that it is she, and she alone, that must gauge and govern the actions that will conclude her desired destiny.

HELENA

Our remedies oft on ourselves do lie,
Which we ascribe to heaven: the fated sky
Gives us free scope, only doth backward pull
Our slow designs when we ourselves are dull.
What power is it which mounts my love so high,
That makes me see, and cannot feed mine eye?
The mightiest space in fortune nature brings
To join like likes and kiss like native things.
Impossible be strange attempts to those
That weigh their pains in sense and do no suppose
What hath been cannot be: who ever strove
To show her merit, that did miss her love?
The king's disease—my project may deceive me,
But my intents are fix'd and will not leave me.

All's Well that Ends Well
COUNTESS—ACT III, SCENE 4

*Bernard Shaw once called the Countess of Rossillion
the best "old lady's part" Shakespeare ever wrote.
Without a doubt, the Countess is a wonderful part,
but there is nothing necessarily "old" about her. She
is a widow and the mother of the present adolescent
count, Bertram, so she has acquired the appellation
Dowager Countess, but this does not mean she's*

*ready for a Bath chair and hot milk. But the Countess
does require an actress of both experience and ability
to portray her striking qualities.*

*The Countess is affectionate, clear-sighted, and
just. She does not let love for her son blind her to his
faults or to his errors; nor does she allow her pride in
her own rank and dignity to shade he perception of
the virtues and the abilities of those lower born than
she, especially the gentlewoman, Helena, whom she
has raised as a daughter; and she is the girl's
protectress. The Countess is, for her time, a true
"democrat."*

*Count Bertram has been forced to marry Helena
by orders of the King of France. Bertram has done so
with great hostility. He has also sent his new wife to
his mother at Rossillion while he steals off to the
wars in Italy. He writes to his wife a devastating letter, renouncing his marriage and outlining
impossible conditions by which he would
acknowledge it. Helena, not to be deterred by such
rejection, has followed, also by stealth, Bertram to
Florence. She has done this by night, leaving a letter
to inform the Countess of her actions. The Countess
is with her household steward, Rynaldo, who has
read the girl's letter to his Lady Countess a number
of times. The Countess is still shaken by Helena's
words.*

COUNTESS

Alas! and would you take the letter of her?
Might you not know she would do as she has done
By sending me a letter?
Ah, what sharp stings are in her mildest words!
Rynaldo, you did never lack advice so much
As letting her pass so; had I spoke with her,
I could have well diverted her intents,
Which thus she hath prevented. What angel shall
Bless this unworthy husband? He cannot thrive,
Unless her prayers, whom heaven delights to hear
And loves to grant, reprieve him from the wrath
Of greatest justice. Write, write, Rynaldo,
To this unworthy husband of his wife;
Let every word weigh heavy on her worth
That he does weigh too light; my greatest grief,
Though little he do feel it, set down sharply.
Dispatch the most convenient messenger.
When haply he shall hear that she is gone,
He will return; and hope I may that she,
Hearing so much, will speed her foot again,
Led hither by pure love. Which of them both
Is dearest to me I have no skill in sense
To make distinction. Provide this messenger.
My heart is heavy and mine age is weak;
Grief would have tears and sorrow bids me speak.

Measure for Measure
ISABELLA—ACT II, SCENE 4

Vincentio, duke of Vienna, has for a brief time turned the reins of government over to his deputy, Lord Angelo, assigning him all of his powers and duties, while the duke "retreats" for meditation. (Secretly, however, the duke remains in the city to see how his government and justice works in his realm.) Lord Angelo is a hard, unbending, and puritanical man. One of his first decrees is to condemn Claudio to death for sleeping with a woman he is unable to marry. Claudio begs his sister, Isabella, a novice in the Order of Ste. Clare, to intercede with Angelo on his behalf. She agrees, and from the first moment he sees her, lust enters Angelo's eyes, mind, heart, and loins. The only way the chaste and good Isabella may "redeem thy brother" is "by yielding up thy body" to Angelo.

Isabella has just endured an interview with Lord Angelo in which he has made the offer he didn't think she would refuse: her body for the life of her brother. But she did refuse, and repels Angelo's advances with a front of her own: if he does not give a pardon to Claudio, she will announce his perfidy to the world. But Angelo has a counter for every threat. Who would believe her, he asks. His "unsoil'd name, the

*austereness of [his] life" would work against her,
and his rank in the State would out weigh her
accusations. Angelo is so put out at Isabella's non-
acquiescence to his demand he tells her that if she
does not submit, not only will Claudio die, but Angelo
will see that it is a death of "lingering sufferance"—
and it will be her fault the way Claudio dies. Angelo
has just left Isabella, giving her twenty-four hours to
return with the expected answer to his demand. She is
alone, except for her goodness and her God.*

ISABELLA

To whom should I complain? Did I tell this,
Who would believe me? O perilous mouths,
That bear in them one and the self-same tongue,
Either of condemnation or approof;
Bidding the law make court'sy to their will;
Hooking both right and wrong to the appetite,
To follow as it draws! I'll to my brother:
Though he hath fall'n by prompture of the blood,
Yet hath he in him such a mind of honour,
That, had he twenty heads to tender down
On twenty bloody blocks, he'ld yield them up,
Before his sister should her body stoop
To such abhorr'd pollution.
Then, Isabel, live chaste, and brother, die:

More than our brother is our chastity.
I'll tell him yet of Angelo's request,
And fit his mind to death, for his soul's rest.

THE HISTORIES

King Henry IV, Part I
LADY PERCY—ACT II, SCENE 3

The two King Henry IV plays are enshrined for their greatest comic creation, Sir John Falstaff, that grand progenitor of numerous humorous types that now abound in dramatic literature. But while the "Henry" plays abound with masculine types, Shakespeare uses the women of the play to humanize the soldier/hero and the braggarts. Lady Percy's brief span upon the stage is an apogee of this use.

Lord Henry Percy, surnamed "Hotspur," is a gallant and brave soldier and a man of honor and honesty, but he is also hot-headed and will jump to action no matter what the consequences. The Percys aided King Henry in his rebellion against King Richard II and had helped Henry gain the crown. Now, they feel they are misused and under-appreciated by the new monarch. Moreover, Hotspur had learned that his brother-in-law, Mortimer, the Earl of March, had been named by Richard II as his heir to the throne. So, Hotspur might have done his own kinsman an injustice by aiding Henry. Hotspur is in a quandary, and he is being pressured to join forces with the Welsh in open rebellion against the king.

Lady Percy is devoted to Hotspur. She is also a
wife in whom her husband mostly confides: they are
friends as well as lovers. But now Hotspur is acting
uncharacteristically toward her. He has closed her
off, is restless, his sleep troubled with dreams, and he
has abandoned their bed. Lady Percy is worried, and
she wants Hotspur to reveal his disquiet to her.

LADY PERCY

O, my good lord, why are you thus alone?
For what offense have I this fortnight been
A banish'd woman from my Harry's bed?
Tell me, sweet lord, what is 't that takes from thee
Thy stomach, pleasure, and thy golden sleep?
Why dost thou bend thine eyes upon the earth,
And start so often when thou sit'st alone?
Why hast thou lost the fresh blood in thy cheeks,
And given my treasures and my rights of thee
To thick-eyed musing and curs'd melancholy?
In thy faint slumbers I by thee have watch'd,
And heard thee murmur tales of iron wars,
Speak terms of manage to thy bounding steed,
Cry, "Courage! To the field!" And thou hast talk'd
Of sallies and retires, of trenches, tents,
Of palisadoes, frontiers, parapets,
Of basilisks, of cannon, culverin,

Of prisoners' ransom, and of soldiers slain,
And all the currents of a heady fight.
Thy spirit within thee hath been so at war,
And thus hath so bestirr'd thee in thy sleep,
That beads of sweat have stood upon thy brow
Like bubbles in a late-disturbed stream,
And in thy face strange motions have appear'd,
Such as we see when men restrain their breath
On some great sudden hest. O, what portents are these?
Some heavy business hath my lord in hand,
And I must know it, else he loves me not.

King Henry IV, Part II
MISTRESS QUICKLY—ACT II, SCENE 1

Mistress Quickly is the "hostess"/proprietress of the Boar's Head Tavern, Eastcheap. This tavern is also the headquarters of Sir John Falstaff and his coterie of dissolute followers. Mistress Quickly speaks plainly and bluntly, but the customers and inhabitants of her establishment are not persons who are managed by soft requests and genteel pleas. Mistress Quickly knows her world and its social order, and she complies as the needs of the occasion demand.

Sir John Falstaff owes Mistress Quickly a goodly sum of money, and to stave off paying her, he has made promises to marry her. However, neither money nor marriage have come forth; so, Mistress Quickly has entered an action in the courts and brought suit against Sir John for breach of both debts. After the proper legal complaints have been registered, Mistress Quickly accompanies two of the Sheriff's officers, Fang and Snare, on their quest to arrest Sir John and to see he's "brought to justice."

MISTRESS QUICKLY

Master Fang, have you entered the action? Where's your yeoman? Is't a lusty yeoman? will a' stand to't? Yea, good Master Snare; I have entered him and all. Alas, the day! take heed of him; he stabbed me in mine own house, and that most beastly: in good faith, he cares not what mischief he does, if his weapon be out: he will foin like any devil; he will spare neither man, woman, nor child. I am undone by his going; I warrant you, he's an infinitive thing upon my score. Good Master Fang, hold him sure: good Master Snare, let him not 'scape. A' comes continuantly to Piecorner—saving your manhoods—to buy a saddle; and he is indited to dinner to the Lubber's-head in Lumbert street, to Master Smooth's the silkman: I pray ye, since my exion is entered and my case so openly known to the world, let him be brought in to his answer. A hundred mark is a long one for a poor lone woman to bear: and I have borne, and borne, and borne, and have been fubbed off, and fubbed off, and fubbed off, from this day to that day, that it is a shame to be thought on. There is no honesty in such dealing; unless a woman should be made an ass and a beast, to bear every knave's wrong. Yonder he comes; and that arrant malmsey-nose knave, Bardolph, with him. Do your offices, do your offices: Master Fang and Master Snare, do me, do me, do me your offices.

King Henry IV, Part II
DOLL TEARSHEET—ACT II, SCENE 4

Victorian writers, in their inestimable way of skirting the sexually obvious, referred to Doll Tearsheet as "a low woman." Another generation would have referred to her as "a woman of easy virtue." Doll is one of those mainstays of dramatic literature from over the centuries: a sympathetic prostitute with a heart of gold. And in the Shakespearean world she is also a woman of character and certain standards; she has her price, but she also has her dignity and moral measures to uphold and to protect. She insists on exerting what control she can over her life and profession.

Mistress Quickly, owner and hostess of the Boar's Head Tavern in Eastcheap, has taken Doll under a sympathetic wing, because Doll has become "sick of a calm" from drinking "Too much canaries; and that's a marvellous searching win. . . ." Into the tavern comes Sir John Falstaff and his retinue of scoundrels, especially one Pistol, Sir John's "ancient" or "ensign." Pistol suffers from that predominantly male point of view that not only is he irresistible, but also that any woman is an easy, capitulating conquest—especially a woman like Doll, who has a notorious business reputation, as her name implies. But Doll does not like Pistol, and she rejects and repels his barrages of verbal innuendoes and lurid assaults. (N.B.—in Elizabethan slang "charge" was usually equated with "to assail sexually.")

DOLL TEARSHEET

Charge me! I scorn you, scurvy companion. What! you poor, base, rascally, cheating, lack-linen mate! Away, you mouldy rogue, away! I am meat for your master. Away, you cut-purse rascal! you filthy bung, away! by this swine I'll thrust my knife in your mouldy chaps, an you play the saucy cuttle with me. Away, you bottle-ale rascal! you basket-hilt stale juggler, you! Since when, I pray you, sir? God's light, with two points on your shoulder? much! Captain! thou abominable damned cheater, art thou not ashamed to be called captain? An captains were of my mind, they would truncheon you out, for taking their names upon you before you have earned them. You a captain! you slave, for what? for tearing a poor whore's ruff in a bawdy-house? He a captain! hang him, rogue! he lives upon mouldy stewed prunes and dried cakes. A captain! God's light, these villains will make the word as odious as the word "occupy"; which was an excellent good word before it was ill sorted: therefore captains had need to look to't. For God's sake, thrust him down stairs; I cannot endure such a fustian rascal.

King Henry V
HOSTESS—ACT II, SCENE 3

Can a heart break? Can a person die of a broken heart? It just might be possible. What we now clinically refer to as "emotional trauma" can lead to physical ailments and breakdowns. After his public repudiation by King Henry V, Sir John Falstaff contracted severe fevers and other ailments which drained the life from him. To on-lookers, they may appear the physical misfortunes of an old reprobate, but Mistress Quickly (the Hostess) knows that "the king has killed his heart."

At the end of King Henry IV, Part II, *Mistress Quickly was in prison on a charge of mayhem, at least, if not possible murder. Some time between then and the events of* King Henry V, *she returns to her tavern in Eastcheap and has married Sir John's ancient (ensign), Pistol. Sir John has also come to the Boar's Head Tavern to die. Mistress Quickly nurses him to the last. This "death of Falstaff" speech is both brief and moving in its simplicity and its charm. What moved Mistress Quickly as she experienced Falstaff's death is what also moves the listeners, Pistol, Nym, and others of Sir John's crew, as the they experience her reliving those last moments in Sir John's life.*

HOSTESS

Nay, sure, he's not in hell: he's in Arthur's bosom, if ever man went to Arthur's bosom. A' made a finer end and went away an it had been any christom child; a' parted even just between twelve and one, even at the turning o' the tide; for after I saw him fumble with the sheets and play with flowers and smile upon his fingers' ends, I knew there was but one way; for his nose was as sharp as a pen, and a' babbled of green fields. "How now, Sir John!" quoth I: "what, man! be o' good cheer." So a' cried out "God, God, God!" three or four times. Now I, to comfort him, bid him a' should not think of God; I hoped there was no need to trouble himself with any such thoughts yet. So a' bade me lay more clothes on his feet: I put my hand into the bed and felt them, and they were as cold as any stone, and so upward and upward, and all was as cold as any stone. For Falstaff he is dead, and we must yearn therefore.

King Henry VI, Part II
QUEEN MARGARET—ACT III, SCENE 2

Margaret of Anjou is married to an imbecilic and weak king in an arrangement made by the man who loves her—a man whose scruples seem to be merely convenient—so that he can be near her; she sees her only son disinherited by his father in favor of her worst enemy and his family; then she experiences the murders of her lover, her son, and her husband; and finally she is thrown down from the heights of power to the ignominity and poverty of a displaced person, harried and crazed by grief and an obsession for revenge. No wonder she is at times unprincipled, vengeful, fierce, audacious, and a virago. She comes to realize she is a woman alone, a woman who must use any means to survive—and to win.

The legendary characteristics of Queen Margaret fascinated Shakespeare. Her dramatic through-line journeys the terrain of four plays, making her character the longest female role in the Shakespearean canon. And, in may ways, Queen Margaret embodies and mirrors the struggle, dissolution, and disintegration of England and its people during the troubled times of The War of the Roses. She makes her first, brief appearance toward the end of King Henry VI, Part I, *as a young, beautiful and seemingly overwhelmed girl. She quickly grows to learn the use of the reins of power and the frustration from being thwarted by lesser men with more authority than "a mere woman" who surround her. And, finally, she is the disoriented, emotionally imbalanced ruin of solid stability and strength she once was. This is also the course of English society during The War of the Roses.*

In King Henry VI, Part II, *Margaret's love affair with the Duke of Suffolk comes into the open. (He is a married man as well; so their situation is impossible.) Suffolk has arranged the murder of King Henry's uncle, the Duke of Gloucester, a political enemy. Gloucester is a highly respected and popular nobleman, Lord Protector of the realm during King*

Henry's long minority, and brother of the late, heroic
King Henry V. But Suffolk's denial that he is in any
way involved in the good duke's death falls on both
deaf and unbelieving ears. The "Commons" (the
people) demand Suffolk's death, but King Henry,
gentle soul that he is, orders Suffolk into a lifetime of
exile. Left alone in the palace chamber with Suffolk,
Queen Margaret faces the inevitable and must bid a
last farewell to the man she passionately loves and
depends on.

QUEEN MARGARET

Enough, sweet Suffolk; thou torment'st thyself;
And these dread curses, like the sun 'gainst glass,
Or like an overcharged gun, recoil,
And turn the force of them upon thyself.
O, let me entreat thee cease. Give me thy hand,
That I may dew it with my mournful tears;
Nor let the rain of heaven wet this place,
To wash away my woeful monuments.
O, could this kiss be printed in thy hand,
That thou mightst think upon these by the seal,
Through whom a thousand sighs are breathed for
thee!
So, get thee gone, that I may know my grief;
'Tis but surmised whiles thou art standing by,

As one that surfeits thinking on a want.
I will repeal thee, or, be well assured,
Adventure to be banished myself:
And banished I am, if but from thee.
Go: speak not to me; even now be gone.
O, go not yet! Even thus two friends condemn'd
Embrace and kiss and take ten thousand leaves,
Loather a hundred times to part than die.
Yet now farewell; and farewell life with thee!

King Henry VI, Part II
QUEEN MARGARET—ACT III, SCENE 2

*The first great, legendary female character of
William Shakespeare's is Margaret of Anjou, queen
to the saintly and imbecilic King Henry VI. She
appears first in Act V, Scene 3 of* King Henry VI, Part
I; *then she is the dominant female character in both*
King Henry VI, Parts II & III; *and she sums up her
career as the dramatically effective "Cassandra," the
mad, deposed Queen Margaret, in* King Richard III.

*Shakespeare's Queen Margaret is coarse, fierce,
revengeful, and unprincipled. Above all, she is
strong. She has to be, for not only is Henry VI a weak
king, he is also a hopeless one; and Margaret is
trying to hold the kingdom together and the throne
for the Lancasterian dynasty. And she is not in love*

with her husband but with the handsome and audacious Duke of Suffolk, who negotiated her marriage. During her reign as queen-consort, Margaret managed to raise armies, lead them to victory and disaster, offend her nobility and her allies, and lose the throne not once but twice, making solid enemies.

Among the early enemies was the Duke of Gloucester, uncle to King Henry. Suffolk arranges the murder of Gloucester, and he then brings the news to the King at Bury St. Edmunds, before the whole court. The King faints at the news, and when Suffolk and the Queen try to comfort him, the King recoils from them in a mad outburst. The Queen is stung by the King's accusation that she is treacherous toward him, or that she was involved in Gloucester's death. She reacts immediately, passionately, and violently—and perhaps just a bit too zealously—in her defense of both herself and Suffolk.

QUEEN MARGARET

Why do you rate my Lord of Suffolk thus?
Although the Duke was enemy to him,
Yet he most Christian-like laments his death.
And for myself, foe as he was to me,
Might liquid tears of heart-offending groans

Or blood-consuming sighs recall his life,
I would be blind with weeping, sick with groans,
Look pale as primrose with blood-drinking sighs,
And all to have the noble Duke alive.
What know I how the world may deem of me?
For it is known we were but hollow friends.
It may be judged I made the Duke away;
So shall my name with slander's tongue be wounded,
And princes' courts be fill'd with my reproach.
This get I by his death. Ay me, unhappy!
To be a queen, and crown'd with infamy!
Be woe for me, more wretched than he is.
What, dost thou turn away and hide thy face?
I am no loathsome leper. Look on me.
What! Art thou, like the adder, waxen deaf?
Be poisonous too, and kill thy forlorn queen.
Is all thy comfort shut in Gloucester's tomb?
Why, then, dame Margaret was ne'er thy joy.
Erect his statue and worship it,
And make my image but an alehouse sign.
Was I for this nigh wrack'd upon the sea
And twice by awkward wind from England's bank
Drove back again unto my native clime?
What boded this, but well forewarning wind
Did seem to say, "Seek not a scorpion's nest,
Nor set no footing on this unkind shore"?
What did I then but cursed the gentle gusts

And he that loos'd them forth their brazen caves,
And bid them blow towards England's blessed shore,
Or turn our stern upon a dreadful rock?
Yet Aeolus would not be a murderer,
But left that hateful office unto thee.
The pretty-vaulting sea refused to drown me,
Knowing that thou wouldst have me drown'd on
shore
With tears as salt as sea, through thy unkindness.
The splitting rocks cowr'd in the sinking sands
And would not dash me with their ragged sides,
Because thy flinty heart, more hard than they,
Might in thy palace perish Margaret.
As far as I could ken thy chalky cliffs,
When from thy shore the tempest beat us back,
I stood upon the hatches in the storm,
And when the dusky sky began to rob
My earnest-gaping sight of thy land's view,
I took a costly jewel from my neck—
A heart it was, bound in with diamonds—
And threw it towards thy land. The sea received it,
And so I wish'd thy body might my heart.
And even with this I lost fair England's view
And bid mine eyes be packing with my heart
And call'd them blind and dusky spectacles,
For losing ken of Albion's wished coast.
How often have I tempted Suffolk's tongue,

The agent of thy foul inconstancy,
To sit and witch me, as Ascanius did
When he to madding Dido would unfold
His father's acts commenced in burning Troy!
Am I not witch'd like her, or thou not false like him?
Ay me, I can no more! Die, Margaret!
For Henry weeps that thou dost live so long.

King Henry VI, Part III
QUEEN MARGARET—ACT I, SCENE 1

Through the years of marriage and reigning, Margaret's nerves have turned raw and she grows more and more infuriated at her husband's incapacity to govern and to rule. At the end of King Henry VI, Part II, *the Yorkists have won the Battle of St. Albans, and, for the time, have the secure upper hand in the on-going War of the Roses. As a compromise, King Henry agrees to make the Duke of York regent of the country, with Henry to retain the titular title of king only for his lifetime. Upon Henry's death, the crown would be inherited by York and his heirs in perpetuity. Henry, in effect, agreed to disinherit his own son, Edward, Prince of Wales, and his future descendants. This action does not sit well with either the prince nor Queen Margaret (and for good reason). This is the action that drives Margaret*

122

*into a final, revengeful fury that leads to all but open
rebellion against her husband and propels forward
the revenge-plot device of* King Henry VI, Part III. *(It
would be rebellion against Henry, except Margaret
becomes head of the Lancasterians against the
Yorkists—i.e., fighting her husband's battles for him
to maintain her son's rights.)*

*Here, Margaret has learned of King Henry's
"compromise" and confronts him. At no time, because of her fury and indignation at this last incapacity of a king that ignites a betrayal by husband and
father, does she consider the appeasement and
reasoning Henry tries to give for his actions.*

QUEEN MARGARET

Nay, go not from me; I will follow thee.
Who can be patient in such extremes?
Ah, wretched man! would I had died a maid,
And never seen thee, never borne thee son,
Seeing thou has proved so unnatural a father!
Hath he deserved to lose his birthright thus?
Hadst thou but loved him half so well as I,
Or felt that pain which I did for him once,
Or nourish'd him as I did with my blood,
Thou wouldst have left thy dearest heart-blood there,
Rather than have made that savage duke thine heir

I shame to hear thee speak. Ah, timorous wretch!
Thou hast undone thyself, thy son and me;
And given unto the house of York such head
As thou shalt reign but by their sufferance.
To entail him and his heirs unto the crown,
What is it, but to make thy sepulchre
And creep into it far before thy time?
Warwick is chancellor and the lord of Calais;
Stern Falconbridge commands the narrow seas;
The duke is made protector of the realm;
And yet shalt thou be safe? Such safety finds
The trembling lamb environed with wolves.
Had I been there, which am a silly woman,
The soldiers should have toss'd me on their pikes
Before I would have granted to that act.
But thou preferr'st thy life before thine honour:
And seeing thou dost, I here divorce myself
Both from thy table, Henry, and thy bed,
Until that act of parliment be repeal'd
Whereby my son is disinherited.
The northern lords that have forsworn thy colours
Will follow mine, if once they see them spread;
And spread they shall be, to thy foul disgrace
And utter ruin of the house of York.
Thus do I leave thee. Come, son, let's away;
Our army is ready; come we'll after them.

[*Exit*]

King Henry VI, Part III
QUEEN MARGARET—ACT V, SCENE 4

The Lancasterian forces have nearly lost The War of the Roses. King Henry is deposed, and the Yorkist heir, Edward, has been crowned King Edward IV. But Margaret and her son, Edward, Prince of Wales, are still in the field with loyal forces. They have recently lost one of the last two decisive battles of the War, the Battle of Barnet, and are about to engage in the last battle, the final Yorkist triumph, the Battle of Tewksbury.

Shakespeare has been very careful in his lengthy portrayal of Margaret: she remains consistant throughout all of the plays, as she is described in this one: "O tiger's heart wrapped in a woman's hide!" She is also motivated by the chief theme of this play: revenge. She does not want just to win, she does not want simply heavenly justice: everything she does is motivated by "Revenge!" (She also knows what lies in store for them if they lose this battle and are captured alive after it.) This is her final attempt to stir her nobles' blood and arouse them for battle—a battle they cannot lose.

QUEEN MARGARET

Great lords, wise men ne'er sit and wail their loss,
But cheerly seek how to redress their harms.
What though the mast be now blown overboard,
The cable broke, the holding-anchor lost,
And half our sailors swallow'd in the flood?
Yet lives our pilot still. Is 't meet that he
Should leave the helm and, like a fearful lad,
With tearful eyes add water to the sea,
And give more strength to that which hath too much,
Whiles, in his moan, the ship splits on the rock,
Which industry and courage might have saved?
Ah, what shame, ah, what a fault were this!
Say Warwick was our anchor; what of that?
And Montague our topmast; what of him?
Our slaughter'd friends the tackles; what of these?
Why, is not Oxford here another anchor?
And Somerset another goodly mast?
The friends of France our shrouds and tacklings?
And, though unskillful, why not Ned and I
For once allow'd the skillful pilot's charge?
We will not from the helm to sit and weep,
But keep our course, though the rough wind say no,
From shelves and rocks that threaten us with wrack.
As good to chide the waves as speak them fair.
And what is Edward but a ruthless sea?

What Clarence but a quicksand of deceit?
And Richard but a ragged fatal rock?
All these the enemies to our poor bark.
Say you can swim; alas, 'tis but a while;
Tread on the sand; why, there you quickly sink:
Bestride the rock; the tide will wash you off,
Or else you famish—that's a threefold death.
This speak I, lords, to let you understand,
If case some one of you would fly from us,
That there's no hoped-for mercy with the brothers
More than with ruthless waves, with sands and rocks.
Why, courage then! What cannot be avoided
'Twere childish weakness to lament or fear.

King Henry VIII
QUEEN KATHERINE—ACT IV, SCENE 2

For nearly twenty-five years, Katherine of Aragon, daughter of Spain's Ferdinand and Isabella, was Queen Consort of England's King Henry VIII. Then she was divorced, annulled, and set aside with the title of Dowager Queen. Queen Katherine, as drawn by Shakespeare, is a proud and strong woman. She takes much pride in her birth and her marriage rank and never waivers from her sense of station. Yet, mingled with these characteristics are qualities of long-enduring affection and a religious humility that blend to create a noble dignity and a gentle pathos of a woman wronged by circumstances. (Another royal woman betrayed by the man or men upon whom she most depends.) Queen Katherine uses these qualities to the very end in her struggle to maintain the position and the rank to which she feels she has the right.

Katherine as Dowager Queen is living in "genteel poverty" (for a queen). She is also in ill-health and she is dying. Her times is short and she knows it. Yet, there is much business to conclude concerning the welfare of her daughter, Mary, and her royal servants. This characteristic of Katherine's, thinking of others even at moments of personal pain and crisis, is what raises her from the merely unfortunate to the noble, dignified lady, wronged by circumstances over which she had no control—nor ever could have had. Katherine's final opportunity to make her worries and wishes known to King Henry comes when she receives a courtesy visit from Capucius, the Spanish ambassador to the English court. (The Spanish king, the Emperor Charles V, is also Katherine's nephew.) Katherine seizes the opportunity to ask Capucius to be her emissary to Henry. She uses her characteristic humility to ask the favor, but underlying the request with regal urgency. In attendance to Katherine, besides Capucius, are Katherine's gentleman-usher, Griffith, and a lady-in-waiting, Patience.

QUEEN KATHERINE

Patience, is that letter,
I caused you write, yet sent away?
Sir, I most humbly pray you to deliver
This to my lord the king.
In which I have commended to his goodness
The model of our chaste loves, his young daughter;
The dews of heaven fall thick in blessings on her!
Beseeching him to give her virtuous breeding,—
She is young, and of a noble modest nature,
I hope she will deserve well,—and a little
To love her for her mother's sake, that loved him,
Heaven knows how dearly. My next poor petition
Is, that his noble grace would have some pity
Upon my wretched women, that so long
Have follow'd both my fortunes faithfully:
Of which there is not one, I dare avow,
And now I should not lie, but will deserve,
For virtue and true beauty of the soul,
For honesty and decent carriage,
A right good husband, let him be a noble:
And, sure, those men are happy that shall have 'em.
The last is, for my men; they are the poorest,
But poverty could never draw 'em from me:
That they may have their wages duly paid 'em,
And something over to remember me by:

If heaven had pleased to have given me longer life
And able means, we had not parted thus.
These are the whole contents: and, good my lord,
But that you love the dearest in this world,
And you wish Christian peace to souls departed,
Stand these poor people's friend, and urge the king
To do me this last right. Remember me
In all humility unto his highness:
Say his long trouble now is passing
Out of this world; tell him, in death I bless'd him,
For so I will. Mine eyes grow dim. Farewell,
My lord. Griffith, farewell. Nay, Patience,
You must not leave me yet: I must to bed;
Call in more women. When I am dead, good wench,
Let me be used with honour: strew me over
With maiden flowers, that all the world may know
I was a chaste wife to my grave: embalm me,
Then lay me forth: although unqueen'd, yet like
A queen, and daughter to a king, inter me.
I can no more.

King Richard II
DUCHESS OF YORK—ACT V, SCENE 3

King Richard II has been deposed as King of England. His cousin, Henry Bolingbroke, has replaced him on the throne as King Henry IV. Richard had to be replaced because he had reached a point where he could not be trusted. The nobles, to survive, had to do something. And because he was the next true male heir in the line of succession to the throne, Bolingbroke was the logical choice to replace Richard. Moreover, Henry was popular with both the nobles and with the people, something Richard was not.

The Duke of York, uncle to both Richard and Henry, has discovered a plot to murder Henry while he's at the tournaments at Oxford. Among the conspirators is York's only son, the Duke of Aumerle. York supports the Crown (whoever is wearing it), even when contrary to his personal/family interests. He is furious at Aumerle, and without hesitation he rides to the King to expose the plot and accuse his son of treason.

Aumerle's mother, the Duchess of York, opposes her husband's action: blood and fatherhood are thicker than treason and regicide. She urges Aumerle to speed to the King ahead of York and to crave the

King's pardon even before *York can arrive to accuse*
him. She then follows them both to make her own plea
to the King.

The scene is the royal palace, where Henry has
first been accosted by a desperate Aurmerle asking
pardon for offenses unknown, which the King grants;
then, by a resolute York, determined to bring his news
and his accusation. And, finally, now by the
distraught Duchess, who does not know what has
gone on before and begs audience. She not only
means to thwart her husband, but also to beseech her
sovereign as a woman for a pardon for her son.

DUCHESS OF YORK

[*Without*]
What ho, my liege! For God's sake, let me in!
Speak with me, pity me, open the door!
A beggar begs that never begg'd before.
    [*Enter Duchess*]
O King, believe not this hard-hearted man!
Love loving not itself, none other can.
Sweet York, be patient. Hear me, gentle liege.
[*Kneels*]
For ever will I walk upon my knees,
And never see day that the happy sees,
Till thou give joy; until thou bid me joy,

By pardoning Rutland, my transgressing boy.
Pleads [York] in earnest? Look upon his face.
His eyes do drop no tears, his prayers are in jest;
His words come from his mouth, ours from our
breast.
He prays but faintly and would be denied;
We pray with heart and soul and all besid.
His weary joints would gladly rise, I know;
Our knees still kneel till to the ground they grow.
His prayers are full of false hypocrisy;
Ours of true zeal and deep integrity.
Our prayers do out-pray his; then let them have
That mercy which true prayer ought to have.
                    Nay, do not say, "stand up."
Say "pardon" first, and afterwards "stand up."
An if I were thy nurse, thy tongue to teach,
"Pardon" should be the first word of thy speech.
I never long'd to hear a word till now;
Say "pardon," King; let pity teach thee how.
The word is short, but not so short as sweet;
No word like "pardon" for kings' mouths so meet.
Speak "pardon" as 'tis current in our land;
The chopping French we do not understand.
Thine eye begins to speak; set thy tongue there,
Or in thy piteous heart plant thou thine ear,
That hearing how our plaints and prayers do pierce,
Pity may move thee "pardon" to rehearse.

I do not sue to stand.

Pardon is all the suit I have in hand.

O happy vantage of a kneeling knee!

Yet am I sick for fear. Speak it again;

Twice saying "pardon" doth not pardon twain,

But makes one pardon strong.

A god on earth thou art.

Come, my old son. I pray God make thee new.

King Richard III
LADY ANNE—ACT I, SCENE 2

*King Richard III is Shakespeare's first great play
and, with the exception of* Hamlet, *the longest of his
plays. It has been a stage favorite from the 1590s to
the present. Actors clamor to do Richard, and actresses long to play Lady Anne. Richard III and
Falstaff seem to have been the two favorite
Shakespearean characters for the Elizabethans.*

*Lady Anne is the first in a line of gentle
Shakespearean women who possess refined grace
and fortitude and are victims of adversity that is not
of their making, not within their control. Desdemona,
Imogen, Hero, and Hermione are among those who
trail in Lady Anne's wake.*

*Lady Anne has every reason to fear, to distrust, to
dislike, and to mourn the actions of the Yorkists. Her*

*father, the powerful kingmaker, the Earl of Warwick,
was wounded in battle against the Yorkists, and he
was left to die on the field of his wounds by the present king, Edward IV. Her husband, Edward, Prince
of Wales, and her father-in-law, King Henry VI, were
both murdered in cold blood with the participation of
Richard. Anne is also the great-great-great grand-
daughter of King Edward III, so her blood is very
blue and her marriage to one of the Yorkists is most
desirable. Richard wants her, but for his own plans.*

*Anne appears in only three scenes, yet she is able
to capture both the imagination and the sympathy of
an audience almost instantaneously. This is her first
entrance in the story. She is the sole mourner for
King Henry VI, and she is following his funeral bier
through the streets of London. She is filled with grief,
but not self-pity, for the fall of the Lancasters.*

LADY ANNE

Set down, set down your honorable load—
If honor may be shrouded in a hearse—
Whilst I awhile obsequiously lament
The untimely fall of virtuous Lancaster.
Poor key-cold figure of a holy king,
Pale ashes of the house of Lancaster,
Thou bloodless remnant of that royal blood,

Be it lawful that I invocate thy ghost
To hear the lamentations of poor Anne,
Wife to thy Edward, to thy slaughter'd son,
Stabb'd by the selfsame hand that made these
wounds!
Lo, in these windows that let forth thy life,
I pour the helpless balm of my poor eyes.
O, cursed be the hand that made these holes!
Cursed the heart that had the heart to do it!
Cursed the blood that let this blood from hence!
More direful hap betide that hated wretch,
That makes us wretched by the death of thee,
Than I can wish to wolves, to spiders, toads,
Or any creeping venom'd thing that lives!
If ever he have child, abortive be it,
Prodigious, and untimely brought to light,
Whose ugly and unnatural aspect
May fright the hopeful mother at the view
And that be heir to his unhappiness!
If ever he have wife, let her be made
More miserable by the death of him
Than I am made by my young lord and thee!
Come, now towards Chertsey with your holy load,
Taken from Paul's to be interred there;
And still, as you are weary of the weight,
Rest you, whiles I lament King Henry's corse.

King Richard III
LADY ANNE—ACT IV, SCENE 1

Among other things, Lady Anne is the widow of Edward, Prince of Wales (son of King Henry VI) whom Richard III helped murder after the battle of Tewkesbury, and she is the daughter of the Earl of Warwick ("the Kingmaker") whom the Yorkists fought and allowed to die unaided at the Battle of Barnet. (The two events happened within a mouth of each other.) Then, with great charm, Richard courted Anne and won her over. But by all indications the marriage (in the play) is anything but a successful one. Lady Anne soon regrets her actions and lives a life of fear, loathing, and misery.

Act IV, Scene 1 is Anne's penultimate appearance in the play. She is escorting her niece, Lady Margaret Plantagenet (the Duke of Clarence's daughter) to the Tower of London to visit the young princes. They meet Queen Elizabeth and the Duchess of York, also on their way to see the princes. The women are denied entry, upon Richard's order; and in the next breath Anne is summoned by Lord Stanley, Earl of Derby, to Westminster, "There to be crowned Richard's royal queen." Thus, altogether, do the women learn of Richard's ascension to the throne. And they all fear at once how he obtained the throne.

Anne, reluctant queen, senses her own dire future as she goes as she is ordered, powerless to do otherwise.

LADY ANNE

Despiteful tidings! O unpleasing news!
And I in all unwillingness will go.
I would to God that the inclusive verge
Of golden metal that must round my brow
Were red-hot steel, to sear me to the brain!
Anointed let me be with deadly venom,
And die, ere men can say, God save the queen!
    When he that is my husband now
Came to me, as I follow'd Henry's corse,
When scarce the blood was well wash'd from his
hands
Issued from my other angel husband
And that dead saint which then I weeping follow'd;
O, when, I say, I look'd on Richard's face,
This was my wish: "Be thou," quoth I, "accursed,
For making me, so young, so old a widow!
And, when thou wed'st, let sorrow haunt thy bed;
And be thy wife—if any be so mad—
As miserable by the life of thee
As thou hast made me by my dear lord's death!"
Lo, ere I can repeat this curse again,
Even in so short a space, my woman's heart

Grossly grew captive to his honey words
And proved the subject of my own soul's curse,
Which ever since hath kept my eyes from rest;
For never yet one hour in his bed
Have I enjoy'd the golden dew of sleep,
But have been waked by timorous dreams.
Besides, he hates me for my father Warwick,
And will, no doubt, shortly be rid of me.

King Richard III
QUEEN MARGARET—ACT IV, SCENE 4

King Richard III has finally ascended the throne. To secure it, he has killed or made to be killed his brother, the Duke of Clarence; his nephews, the young King Edward V and the young Duke of York; Lord Hastings, the Lord Chancellor; Queen Elizabeth's brother and son, Earl Rivers and Lord Grey (respectively); and Sir Thomas Vaughan—not to mention that he also killed King Henry VI and his son, Edward, Prince of Wales; and he may have had a hand in hastening the death of his other brother, King Edward IV. Since his coronation, Richard has caused his cohort in crime, the Duke of Buckingham, to go into rebellion and then to execution. Richard has also poisoned his wife, Lady Anne, so that he may marry his own child-niece, the daughter of Edward IV.

Looming ominously at the side of all this perfidy is the haggard and deposed Queen Margaret, widow of Henry VI. She is not thought much of a threat anymore because she moves freely within the palaces and among the reigning family. She is worn and pressed by her life and losses, but she has never, never lost her thirst for revenge. She is powerless now, without base or battle-axe, so she can only fight with curses pronounced on her enemies and spout Cassandra-like prophecies.

Here the old dragon joins Richard's mother, the Dowager Duchess of York, and his sister-in-law, the Dowager Queen Elizabeth, in lamenting where their family wars have delivered them and their country, whose prosperity and safety was charged to their keep.

QUEEN MARGARET

So, now prosperity begins to mellow
And drop into the rotten mouth of death.
Here in these confines slily have I lurk'd,
To watch the waning of mine enemies.
And will to France, hoping the consequence
Will prove as bitter, black, and tragical.

[*Approaching Queen Elizabeth and the Duchess of York*]

If ancient sorrow be most reverend,
Give mine the benefit of seniory,
And let my griefs frown on the upper hand.
If sorrow can admit society.

[*Sitting down with them*]

Tell o'er your woes again by viewing mine:
I had an Edward, till a Richard kill'd him;
I had a Harry, till a Richard kill'd him;
Thou hadst an Edward, till a Richard kill'd him;
Thou hadst a Richard, till a Richard kill'd him.
Thou hadst a Clarence too, and Richard kill'd him.
From forth the kennel of thy womb hath crept
A hell-hound that doth hunt us all to death.
That dog, that had his teeth before his eyes
To worry lambs and lap their gentle blood,
The foul defacer of God's handiwork,
That excellent grand tyrant of the earth
That reigns in galled eyes of weeping souls,
Thy womb let loose, to chase us to our graves.
O upright, just, and true-disposing God,
How do I thank thee, that this carnal cur
Preys on the issue of his mother's body,
And makes her pew-fellow with others' moan!
Bear with me. I am hungry for revenge,
And now I cloy me with beholding it.

141

Thy Edward he is dead, that kill'd my Edward;
Thy other Edward is dead, to quit my Edward;
Young York he is but boot, because both they
Match'd not the high perfection of my loss.
Thy Clarence he is dead that stabb'd my Edward;
And the beholders of this frantic play,
The adulterate Hastings, Rivers, Vaughan, Grey,
Untimely smother'd in their dusky graves.
Richard yet lives, hell's black intelligencer,
Only reserved their factor to buy souls
And send them thither: but at hand, at hand,
Ensues his piteous and unpitied end.
Earth gapes, hell burns, fiends roar, saints pray,
To have him suddenly convey'd from hensce
Cancel his bond of life, dear God, I pray,
That I may live to say, The dog is dead!

King John
CONSTANCE—ACT III, SCENE 1

*King John is strictly an Elizabethan chronicle play;
and it has never been very popular, perhaps because
of its style (which harkens back to pageant plays and
to formal tableaux). The play, however, is peopled
with dramatic and sympathetic and sinister
characters. Some of the passages are eloquently
written, stirring, and moving.*

142

Constance is a dramatically effective character; one of Shakespeare's most imaginative, impassioned, and eloquent women. She is the widow of Geoffrey Plantagenet, third son of King Henry II and younger brother of King Richard I (Coeur-de-lion). Geoffrey pre-deceased Richard, and Richard had named Geoffrey's son, Arthur, his heir in 1190. Before Arthur can claim the throne on the death of his uncle, his other uncle, and Richard's youngest brother, John, produced a later will that named him heir before Arthur. Arthur at this time is still a minor, so Constance is fighting for his claim—intent to use force, if necessary, to gain England by allying herself with France and Austria. Constance's whole life is dominated by her love for Arthur and her ambitions for him. She is not much principled nor does she entertain much fairness of mind when it comes to his rights and claims to the English throne.

She is a well-developed character who progresses through the play from a forlorn widow's state to one of apprehension, then to states of anger and resentment as the betrayal of her son (and herself) and his cause by the various monarchs evolves. Constance reacts against all the "trafficking and bargaining" with a natural resentment. Finally, she is driven crazy with grief when Arthur falls into the hands of King John.

The powers of England and France have met be-
fore the city of Angiers, with inconclusive results. But
the truce terms are by no means inconclusive. In
return for withdrawing their support to Arthur's
claim to the English throne, John gives France his
niece in marriage to the French Dauphin, Lewis, and
as her dowry returns five rich French provinces. John
offers as consolation to make Arthur Duke of
Brittany, which he already is, and Lord of Angiers. A
poor substitute for a crown and an empire.

The Earl of Salisbury has just delivered the news
of the truce and the marriage to Constance and
Arthur. He has also been instructed to escort them to
the two kings.

CONSTANCE

Gone to be married? gone to swear peace?
False blood to false blood join'd! gone to be friends?
Shall Lewis have Blanch, and Blanch those provinces?
It is not so; thou has misspoke, misheard.
Be well advised, tell o'er thy tale again.
It cannot be; thou dost but say 'tis so.
I trust I may not trust thee, for thy word
Is but the vain breath of a common man.
Believe me, I do not believe thee, man;

144

I have a king's oath to the contrary.
Thou shalt be punish'd for thus frighting me,
For I am sick and capable of fears,
Oppress'd with wrongs, and therefore full of fears,
A widow, husbandless, subject to fears,
A woman, naturally born to fears;
And though thou now confess thou didst but jest,
With my vex'd spirits I cannot take a truce,
But they will quake and tremble all this day.
What dost thou mean by shaking of thy head?
Why dost thou look so sadly on my son?
What means that hand upon that breast of thine?
Why holds thy eye that lamentable rheum,
Like a proud river peering o'er his bounds?
Be these sad signs confirmers of thy words?
Then speak again—not all thy former tale,
But this one word, whether thy tale be true.
O, if thou teach me to believe this sorrow,
Teach thou this sorrow how to make me die,
And let belief and life encounter so
As doth the fury of two desperate men
Which in the very meeting fall and die.
Lewis marry Blanch! O boy, then where art thou?
France friend with England, what becomes of me?
France is a bawd to Fortune and King John,
That strumpet Fortune, that usurping John!
Tell me, thou fellow, is not France forsworn?

Envenom him with words, or get thee gone
And leave those woes alone which I alone
Am bound to underbear. I will not go with thee.
I will instruct my sorrows to be proud,
For grief is proud and makes his owner stoop.
To me and to the state of my great grief
Let kings assemble, for my grief's so great
That no supporter but the huge firm earth
Can hold it up. Here I and sorrows sit;
Here is my throne, bid kings come bow to it.

King John
CONSTANCE—ACT III, SCENE 1

*Constance is another in Shakespeare's line of royal
women who is betrayed by the men surrounding her,
and upon whom she depends. Constance is the widow
of Geoffery Plantagenet, younger brother of Richard
I. Geoffery pre-deceased Richard, and in 1190
Richard named Geoffery's and Constance's son,
Arthur, as his heir to the throne of England. Before
Arthur, who is a minor, can claim the throne, his
other uncle, John (Richard's youngest brother),
produces a later will in which he is named heir over
Arthur. Constance wages a continual struggle—by
force if necessary by allying herself with France and*

Austria—to secure her son's rights and gain recognition to his claims to the English throne.

Armies from England and France have met before the city of Angiers. The battle results are inconclusive but the negotiated terms of peace are far from inconclusive. By terms of the truce, King John agrees to marry his niece, Blanch, to the French Dauphin, Lewis, and cede five rich provinces back to France as her dowry. In return France (and her allies) will withdraw their support to Arthur's claims to the English throne. Constance's reaction to all of this "trafficking and bargaining" is a forceful and natural resentment. She and her son have been betrayed for political expediency. Immediately after being informed of the terms of the treaty, Constance confronts King John, King Philip of France, and Lymoges, Duke of Austria, in the camp of the French.

CONSTANCE

What hath this day deserved? what hath it done,
That it in golden letters should be set
Among the high tides in the calendar?
Nay, rather turn this day out of the week,
This day of shame, opression, perjury,
Or, if it must stand still, let wives with child
Pray that their burthens may not fall this day,

Lest that their hopes prodigiously be cross'd:
But on this day let seamen fear no wreck;
No bargains break that are not this day made:
This day, all things begun come to ill end,
Yea, faith itself to hollow falsehood change!
You have beguiled me with a counterfeit
Resembling majesty, which, being touch'd and tried,
Proves valueless: you are forsworn, forsworn;
You came in arms to spill mine enemies blood,
But now in arms you strengthen it with yours:
The grappling vigour and rough frown of war
Is cold in amity and painted peace,
And our opression hath made up this league.
Arm, arm you heavens, against these perjured kings!
A widow cries: be husband to me, heavens!
Let not the hours of this ungodly day
Wear out the day in peace; but, ere sunset,
Set armed discord 'twixt these perjured kings!
Hear me, O, hear me!
War! War! no peace! peace is to me a war.
O Lymoges! O Austria! thou does shame
That bloody spoil; thou slave, thou wretch, thou
coward!
Thou little valiant, great in villany!
Thou ever strong upon the stronger side!
Thou Fortune's champion that dost never fight
But when her humorous ladyship is by

To teach thee safety! thou are perjured too,
And soothest up greatness. What a fool art thou,
A ramping fool, to brag and stanp and swear
Upon my party! Thou cold-blodded slave,
Hath thou not spoke like thunder on my side,
Been sworn my soldier, bidding me depend
Upon my stars, thy fortune and thy strength,
And dost thou now fall over my foes?
Thou wear a lion's hide! doff it for shame,
And hang a calf's-skin on those recreant limbs.

King John
CONSTANCE—ACT III, SCENE 4

Right upon the heels of the newly established peace
between England and France, Pandulph, the papal
legate, arrives. John has defied the Pope by blocking
the installment of Stephen Langton as Archbishop of
Canterbury. As a result, John is excommunicated.
Pandulph charges France to "desert England" and
to become the "champion of our church," or France
stands to be excommunicated as well.

In the ensuing war, France loses. Arthur is cap-
tured by John and is taken to England by force. His
fate is unknown, but suspected. Constance knows
what will happen to her son in England. Deserted,
distraught, desperate, deranged, Constance confronts

King Philip of France, the Dauphin Lewis, and Pandulph.

CONSTANCE

Lo, now! Now see the issue of your peace.
No, I defy all counsel, all redress,
But that which ends all counsel, true redress,
Death, death. O amiable, lovely death,
Thou odoriferous stench! Sound rottenness,
Arise forth from the couch of lasting night,
Thou hate and terror to prosperity,
And I will kiss thy detestable bones,
And put my eyeballs in thy vaulty brows,
And ring these fingers with thy household worms,
And stop this gap of breath with fulsome dust,
And be a carrion monster like thyself.
Come, grin on me, and I will think thou smil'st,
And buss thee as thy wife. Misery's love,
O, come to me!
O, that my tongue were in the thunder's mouth!
Then with a passion would I shake the world,
And rouse from sleep that fell anatomy
Which cannot hear a lady's feeble voice,
Which scorns a modern invocation.
Thou are not holy to belie me so.
I am not mad. This hair I tear is mine;

My name is Constance; I was Geoffrey's wife;
Young Arthur is my son, and he is lost.
I am not mad; I would to heaven I were!
For then, 'tis like I should forget myself.
O, if I could, what grief should I forget?
Preach some philosophy to make me mad,
And thou shall be canonized, Cardinal;
For being not mad, but sensible of grief,
My reasonable part produces reason
How I may be deliver'd of these woes,
And teaches me to kill or hang myself.
If I were mad, I should forget my son,
Or madly think a babe of clouts were he.
I am not mad. Too well, too well I feel
The different plague of each calamity.
I tore [hair] from their bonds, and cried aloud
"O that these hands could so redeem my son,
As they have given these hairs their liberty!"
But now I envy at their liberty,
And will again commit them to their bonds,
Because my poor child is a prisoner.
And, father Cardinal, I have heard you say
That we shall see and know our friends in heaven.
If that be true, I shall see my boy again;
For since the birth of Cain, the first male child,
To him that did but yesterday suspire,
There was not such a gracious creature born.

But now will canker sorrow eat my bud
And chase the native beauty from his cheek,
And he will look as hollow as a ghost,
As dim and meagre as an ague's fit,
And so he'll die; and, rising so again,
When I shall meet him in the court of heaven
I shall not know him. Therefore never, never
Must I behold my pretty Arthur more.
Grief fills the room up of my absent child,
Lies in his bed, walks up and down with me,
Puts on his pretty looks, repeats his words,
Remembers me of all his gracious parts,
Stuffs out his vacant garments with his form;
Then, have I reason to be fond of grief?
Fare you well! Had you such a loss as I,
I could give better comfort than you do.
I will not keep this form upon my head,
When there is such disorder in my wit.
O Lord! My boy, my Arthur, my fair son!
My life, my joy, my food, my all the world!
My widow-comfort, and my sorrows' cure!

       [*Exit*]